WILD BRANCH ON THE OLIVE TREE

A priest from the Irish countryside and a rabbi from a Russian ghetto prove—through dramatic dialogue and compelling photography—that Jewish-Christian understanding can become a way of life. Father William Treacy and Rabbi Raphael Levine first met in 1960, when they became panel members on *Challenge*, a TV service program featuring a Protestant, a Catholic and a Jew. Weekly for 14 years, *Challenge* received prime television time. Father Treacy and Rabbi Levine became permanent members and their friendship ripened and deepened.

Wild Branch on the Olive Tree tells the life and background of these men "behind the panel." Part One is the priest's; Part Two, the rabbi's. Each tells about his life and work—the priest from his birth in Laoighis County, Ireland, up to the present. Rabbi Levine comes on in Part Two with stories of his hardships as a boy in a Polish village, through his years as attorney, then rabbi. The stories overlap and complement each other; and they abound in many a heartwarming anecdote and human interest story.

We see how Father Treacy and Rabbi Levine, in public forum and private seminar, have disputed, argued and opposed, but always with open mind. They come to grips on major issues but show how even persons with deep differences on fundamental issues can have respect for the convictions of others. This, it would appear, is religion at its best, and the basis of true democracy.

You will find *Wild Branch on the Olive Tree* marvelously human and direct; its candor, disarming. Both the rabbi and the priest write with the same eager enthusiasm that marked their TV programs, to the delight of thousands of viewers.

D1010839

Wild Branch on the Olive Tree

Special Limited Edition

William Tracy

Raphael H Levine

Wild Branch on

by

Father William Treacy and Rabbi Raphael Levine

in collaboration with
Sister Patricia Jacobsen

All the branches are holy if the root is holy. No doubt some of the branches have been cut off, and, like shoots of wild olive, you have been grafted among the rest to share with them the rich sap provided by the olive tree itself, but still, even if you think yourself superior to the other branches, remember that you do not support the root; it is the root that supports you.

(St. Paul's letter to the Romans 11:16-19)

2536 S.E. Eleventh • Portland, Oregon 97242

the Olive Tree

Binford & Mort
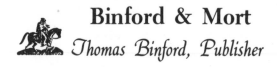
Thomas Binford, Publisher

Dedication

To a better understanding between peoples of all races, colors and faiths, recognizing our basic unity as children of one God and with the deep conviction that we are brothers in our common humanhood, this book is humbly dedicated.

Foreword

I feel privileged to be asked by Rabbi Levine and Father Treacy to write one of the forewords, particularly since the other foreword is written by the erudite theologian and ecumenist, Father Edward H. Flannery.

My brief comments are based upon my personal association and work with Rabbi Levine and Father Treacy. My remarks are also colored by my own background and experience as an American Jew. I grew up on a row-house neighborhood in Philadelphia, Pennsylvania. The area was mainly Irish Catholic and on my own city block the three connecting houses produced a Jesuit priest, a nun and a rabbi.

I must also state that it was a very maturing experience for me to be a professor of history at a fine Catholic college—King's College in Wilkes Barre, Penna. for seven years.

My words then, are predicated on my life experiences, observations and deep feelings for the gentlemen who wrote this book and their life-style.

The Jewish New Year tells us that God created one world on Rosh Hashonah. Being egocentric we believe that God's greatest creation was man. We truly believe that with the human capacity to comprehend, understand, love and help build a better world that God's work was marvelous and awesome.

The relationship the authors have established proves the ultimate in a "heaven here on earth" philosophy. Just as there are dark clouds, rain, sleet, snow and storms in the sky, so their relationship has had trials, disagreements and misunderstandings. But they have grown as men, spiritual leaders, community giants and their bond of friendship has been forged and strengthened in the fiery trials of life and work.

The Brotherhood road has not always been smooth. We basically agree on ethics and morality, but in theology we obviously differ. Brotherhood has also been shaken in recent years by socio-economic and geo-political influences. For years we were all too insecure to talk about our differences, and thus we stressed similarities and sameness. Today, not only can we, but we must be able to face each other with openness and honesty that will lead to understanding and respect. The Rabbi and Priest have shown us in their lives and deep and real friendship that agreement and conformity are not necessary in every instance.

The book is a combination of their thoughts, accomplishments, philosophies, hopes and dreams. It is a sincere and often brilliant effort to inspire and help us to seek truth even if it does not fit our preconceived ideas. They successfully teach us that words, true dialogue can make strangers into friends and friends into co-workers building a world where peace and brotherhood will be more than orator's phrases.

These preachers have lived a sermon of exquisite beauty that they have been kind enough to share with us because they know that platitudes will not bring us together or solve the deeper problems of ecumenism, but that patience and practice will help reduce tensions, and togetherness will be more than fancy phrases and phony facades.

Rabbi Levine and Father Treacy have proven in their pages and problem solving lines, that God has touched each of us with a spark of divinity. They are true servants of the Living God who wish us to lead happier, fuller, more beautiful and more meaningful lives. They believe we can do this and they pass their heritage on in this volume. May the words of their mouths and the prayers of their hearts become the work of our hands.

Dr. Earl Starr
Senior Rabbi, Temple De Hirsch Sinai

Seattle, Washington
October 1974

Foreword

It is widely conceded that since the Six-Day War of 1967 Christian-Jewish relations have slackened. Many on both the Christian and Jewish side of the dialogue have been disappointed by the failure of the churches and synagogues to press more vigorously for implementation of their basic statements or avowals of commitment to the cause of Jewish-Christian understanding. Even more realistic observers are not fully satisfied with the progress more recently made.

Against this sobering backdrop of partially unfulfilled hopes Fr. Treacy and Rabbi Levine's *Wild Branch on the Olive Tree* comes on the scene as a pure delight to the Jewish-Christian ecumenist.

It would be easy to underestimate the book. Structurally, stylistically, it makes no pretenses. It presents no radically new insights or ways to achieving Jewish-Christian harmony. And yet in its simplicity and charm it contrasts favorably with many more elaborate analyses of the problems of Jewish-Christian amity.

This unembellished story of the backgrounds, collaboration, and friendship of a priest from the Irish countryside and a Rabbi from a Russian ghetto is the best proof that the reconciliation, more, the embrace of Christian and Jew is not only possible, but the natural and inevitable outgrowth of interreligious efforts.

The association of Rabbi Levine and Father Treacy provides a model of "flesh and blood" ecumenism, that brand of personal encounter across widely separated cultures and beliefs that gets beyond the "ecumenical smile" and other such niceties to involve the participants in a loving and ennobling human symbiosis. Beyond all theological and sociological inquiries, this approach must be viewed as the ultimate aim of the Jewish-Christian dialogue.

This interpretation of the book need not detract from the intellectual elements of the book, its authors —or of the Christian-Jewish dialogue. The tough issues are not absent from the Rabbi and the priest's projects and discussions, and are always well thought out. This is no easy, sentimental association. Both authors are well trained in theology and are acutely aware of the problems and issues that divide and join the Christian and Jewish traditions. Seasoned ecumenists will learn from this rich association of these two godly men of action.

The final message of *Wild Branch on the Olive Tree* is a simple but important one: The *via regia* to ecumenical achievement is found in intensive personal contact. Rabbi Levine and Father Treacy speak of their relation as a father-son one. It is a familial parameter, and it is on such a level of relation that interreligious encounter will thrive. Intellectual expertise enhances such encounters but can never replace them.

Father Edward H. Flannery
Executive Secretary
Secretariat for Catholic-Jewish Relations
Bishops' Committee for Ecumenical and
*   Interreligious Affairs*

Washington, D.C.
August 1974

Contents

Part One — Father Treacy

Part Two — Rabbi Levine

Epilogue — Father Treacy

Acknowledgment

It is difficult to recall everyone who has had some meaningful influence in the writing of this book. There are so many to whom we owe debts of gratitude for their advice, help and inspiration. However outstanding among them all is Arthur Gerbel, the Public Affairs director of TV Station KOMO who first approached us on behalf of the management with the idea of a TV panel program in 1960. To him and the management of KOMO TV, for their faith in us and for their wholehearted cooperation throughout the fourteen years of our association with them, giving the program prime TV time as a public service 52 weeks of the year and re-broadcasting it also during the week both on TV and radio, thus giving it unusual exposure, we are immeasurably grateful. Among them we cannot refrain from mentioning Mr. William Warren, President of KOMO who suggested the title *Challenge* and for his unfailing faith in us. To Dorothy Sortor Stimson, our producer for the first two years and for Mrs. James Wilson, "Mother Marty" as we affectionately called her, for she mothered us indeed for the next eleven years, to Ken Ritchie, our sensitive and creative director throughout all these years, to Don McCune, who was not only our announcer but a most creative writer who set the tone and the theme of every program with delicate sensitivity and insight, and Tim Bullard who succeeded Arthur Gerbel on his retirement as Public

Affairs Director and carried on the fine work of his predecessor.

To our Protestant colleagues on Challenge, Dr. Martin Goslin of the Plymouth Congregational Church who served as the first Protestant panelist for two years until he left Seattle for a post in St. Louis, Missouri, Dr. Lynn Corson, Senior Minister of the University Methodist Temple who was our second panelist for six years until he left for California and has since died, to Pastor Oscar Rolander who succeeded him two years later until he was called by his Church to Geneva, Switzerland to preside over the Church's missionary work in Tanzania, Africa and is presently serving as pastor of Andrews Lutheran Church of the Redeemer in Bellevue, Washington. He was succeeded by Dr. Robert Fine, minister of the Pacific University Free Methodist Church of Seattle.

To these we add David Crocket, program director of KOMO TV, who saw the potentials of the program and gave it his unstinting support and his successor Edward Lackner and the entire production staff and crew who helped to make the weekly program of Challenge not only just another TV show but the institution it became to tens of thousands of viewers throughout the Pacific Northwest including British Columbia across these fourteen years. A word of special thanks to Joseph Scaylea, artist photographer of the Seattle Times and to Willard Hatch, KOMO Photographer, for their gracious permission to use the beautiful photographs appearing on the cover and elsewhere in this book. Also to Father Edward Flannery, author of the "Anguish of the Jews", director of the Secretariat of Catholic-Jewish Relations, and to Dr. Earl Starr, Senior Rabbi of Temple De Hirsch Sinai, for their generous forewords.

We were unable to determine the names of the many photographers, both of the Seattle Times and of the Seattle Post Intelligencer, but we wish to acknowledge the wonderful cooperation we received from both of our daily newspapers at all times.

To all those mentioned we acknowledge gratefully our loyal weekly audience for their encouraging letters and sometimes their creative criticism which helped us to make Challenge more fully responsive to their needs.

These words of acknowledgment would be incomplete without expressing our immeasurable debt to Sister Patricia Jacobsen, our collaborator, without whose dedicated and tireless work across the past three years, typing and retyping the manuscript, editing and at times rewriting portions of it, thus putting it into the form which made the book publishable.

Wild Branch on the Olive Tree

Part One

FATHER TREACY

1

The Rabbi—Matchmaker for the Priest

I am a Catholic priest for 30 years, in good standing with my Church. How, in heaven's name, can I have a rabbi as matchmaker?

It is the story of an Irish farm boy becoming a priest, coming to the United States on a troopship in time of war 1945, and of a rabbi born in a Jewish ghetto in Russian-occupied Vilna, Lithuania, who traveled in steerage to the United States with his parents at the age of seven, became a lawyer, then was ordained a rabbi and served in Liverpool and London until the German blitz forced him to leave. He arrived in Seattle in 1942.

I met the former lawyer and rabbi for the first time in 1960 and together we launched a weekly television program that continued for 14 years in the Pacific Northwest. This rabbi has changed my life more than anyone else I have met. I trust and honor him as a father.

One evening during a TV discussion on marriage, the Rabbi jokingly said to me, "Father, I know you and I know women. If you ever decide to get married, let me know and I will select a wife for you!"

In Judaism a married priesthood was the norm. Most of the prophets were married. The tradition of an unmarried priesthood does not have its roots in Judaism but in Christianity. A measure of the growth in my relationship with the Rabbi and of our religious understanding is our ability to discuss a subject like

1

celibacy, its demands, dangers and fulfillment as I have experienced them, a way of life with which the Rabbi was unacquainted until we met.

Celibacy for the priest is a commitment to love and serve mankind with all his being, a choice not to marry in order to be more fully available to all men. It is a choice many people find hard to understand, like the young G.I. I once shared a taxi with shortly after his return from war in Europe. He had never spoken to a priest before and his first question startled me: "Why don't you marry?" I explained the demands of the priesthood and the freedom needed to meet those demands, relating this to what his country in war asked of him in leaving his wife and family. He countered with, "I always looked at it differently. To me you are a man out-of-step who deliberately remains that way and has constantly to convince himself of his reasons for being different." I have often thought about what the young man said and while I may be out-of-step with life-styles most commonly accepted as normal, I think it is quite possible to be so and not be out-of-step with life itself at its deepest. And a lifetime of living celibacy has firmly convinced me that it can be a powerful life-giving force. Ratified at the time of ordination, it is a commitment that as in marriage has to be renewed many times in life because at the time it is made its full demands cannot be foreseen.

Relationships of friendship and love between a priest and other people are subject to the same dangers and difficulties that people generally have to face in friendship and love, whether married or not. One's faith in a friend can be lost and its loss can be the death of love and friendship in or out of marriage. The discovery of failings and flawed character can precipitate a crisis and a choice: to feel betrayed and become discouraged at the effort to love, and write off the unloving, warped personality; or to make a new commitment to loving the other, trusting in the ability of both to grow. It is when we make the latter choice that love becomes redeeming and Christ-like; it becomes life-giving. Renewed faith in oneself and in another impels toward growth and fuller life. Rabbi and I have known the other's failings on many occasions and our friendship is stronger for it. He has seen my anger and I have had to adjust to what he calls his "high" and "low" moods.

The priest preoccupied with preserving his vow of celibacy in its narrowest sense closes himself to others and can easily yield to the temptation to flee the pains and problems of love and give up the effort to love, especially where women are concerned, on the grounds of safety. And yet because he is ordained to continue the loving ministry of Jesus, he must seek to know the height and depth of the love of Jesus, a love which he recalls especially every time he offers Mass. Love for people took Jesus from safe paths to walk the Via Dolorosa scourged and crowned with thorns to an agonizing death on a cross. If I seek to walk in His footsteps, I must expect contradictions, complexity and pain as well as joy in human relationships, remembering how Jesus was attacked for His friendship with individuals.

This is the theology of love expressed in Christian terms as I see it and a fitting introduction to *Wild Branch on the Olive Tree*, for it is the basis for my priesthood and for my relationship with the Rabbi. Rabbi and I have often discussed the reality behind this theology and he has never had any difficulty in understanding the details of relationships in the life of his celibate Christian colleague. Because of our mutual trust I found that as time went on I could open my heart to him as to a father confessor and confide to him struggles as a priest of a very personal nature.

And as our friendship grew, he came to understand not only the vocation to celibate priesthood but also the vocation of the Catholic nun who made the choice to serve God in the single state. Until very recently priests and nuns followed their separate paths of service in the Church and there was little of the personal, little or nothing in the way of friendship between them. Happily, a closer partnership is developing as they see each other sharing a beautiful vision of life that includes death and that trusts beyond it. They realize that in following their Christian vocation in a celibate life, they do not have to fear each other, that contributions to the Church and the world are immeasurably enriched by what men and women are able to contribute to one another's consciousness and sensitivity, that valuing another's commitment is a part of what love is.

One person who helped the Rabbi to appreciate celibacy and its implications is a woman I met in September 1947. She had just graduated in journalism from Washington State University and had come to talk with me about her desire to be a foreign missionary. Her father was a Scandinavian Lutheran, later Presbyterian; her mother, an Irish Catholic. Her name was Patricia Jacobsen. She was raised on a farm in Lewis County, Washington, and had never attended a Catholic school or even talked with a Catholic sister. In 1948 she joined the Maryknoll Sisters, founded in this century mainly for overseas work. She was sent to Hong Kong and during the 16 years she was there, we met only twice when she came home on furlough. We kept in close touch by letter and followed one another's activities, thinking and growth. In 1970 she returned to Seattle for two years to study for a master's degree in communications at the University of Washington and is now at Maryknoll headquarters in New York. She was of invaluable assistance in editing and typing this book.

When we started the book, I introduced her to the "Match-maker" and he has come to cherish her as a very special friend. The three of us have had many discussions on many subjects together including whether or not we would be able to work more effectively in God's service with the help and support of marriage. Rabbi acknowledged that while he thought we could bring immeasurable strength and enrichment to the living out of our religious vocations if we were married, he had come to know how much our faith means to us, how much support we are able to give one another within the disciplines of that faith, how in being true to the best in ourselves, we are bringing out the best in one another.

We have come to know how closeness of mind and heart can grow despite physical separation. The Austrian psychiatrist, Viktor Frankl, a Jew imprisoned in Auschwitz during World War II, learned much about love in the concentration camp. He studied the reactions of his fellow inmates to the inhuman conditions they had to face. He saw the power of love to give physical and emotional strength when loved ones were separated from one another. All during the war, though separated from his wife, the knowledge of her love sustained him. In *The Doctor and The Soul*, he writes: "Love is independent of the body to the extent that it does not need the body. Even in love between the sexes the body, the sexual element, is not primary; it is not an end in itself but a means of expression. Love as such can exist without it. When sexual expression is possible, love will desire and seek it; but where renunciation is called for, love will not necessarily cool or die. The spiritual self takes form in giving shape to its psychic and physical modes of appearance and expression. Loving represents a coming to relationship with another as a spiritual being."

My friendship with Sister Patricia Jacobsen is one of the best gifts that God has given to me and a confirmation in my life of what Frankl wrote. From this friendship has come a clearer understanding of my own vocation as priest and a deeper commitment to the teachings of Jesus in which total commitment to our vocation is rooted.

One of Ireland's greatest priests was Canon Sheehan who expressed much of his philosophy through novels. In *Geoffrey Austin*, published at the beginning of this century, he wrote: "It has been said often and let me repeat it for the 100th time that the best grace a young man can receive in life is the friendship of a good woman. And there is no clearer indication of the depths of vulgarity and degradation into which we have fallen than the universal idea that there can be no such friendship between man and woman that does not sooner or later degenerate into sensuous affection. The universal presumption that marriage is the 'be all' and 'end all' of woman's life tends to enervate natures that are of themselves strong and reliant. And thousands of women who as their labors in hospitals and on battlefields can testify, might be the props and supports of weary or broken spirits become the merest parasites living in the weak presumption that they must find the oak around which they can cling and rest or perish. It is impossible to calculate the loss to humanity resulting from this false and unnatural view. It is impossible to calculate the heart suffering and martyrdom of women who believe they can have only one vocation in life and whose views of men are restricted to that one idea." [1]

---

(1) A man with another prophetic vision at the beginning of this century was Dr. F.U. Foerster of the University of Zurich, Department of Psychology. He was not a Catholic. In *Marriage and the Sex Problem*, he wrote: "The oath of voluntary celibacy, so far from degrading marriage, is a support to the holiness of the marriage bond, since it gives material shape to the spiritual freedom of man in the face of natural impulses."

There have been many instances when a special love has entered my life or entered the lives of others for me, as happens in the life of the priest in every country and culture. Love makes us weak, gives others power over us and sometimes that power is used cruelly. Love gives joy but it also means pain and separation. The Christian with his easter outlook does not accept any separation as final and knows that true love cannot be terminated even by death. Holding on to that vision with another, renewing it, living with the darkness, waiting for the light together, is to experience life at its best.

Commitment to priesthood has taken me along roads not too well marked where I have known agonizing fear and uncertainty, roads not drawn in the Maynooth map of life given to me in seminary days. Many people by their love have helped me to grow in love—parents, priests, people I introduce in this book and many others. In my relationship with the Rabbi and these many others I have come to a new understanding of God's revelation to us—that it is safe to love.

The pages that follow reveal more of the Irish farm boy and priest who presented himself to the Rabbi in 1960 to begin a career together on television and a friendship that grows deeper and stronger as the years go on. I can honestly say that I love him as a father who by his patience, insights and love has raised me to be a better priest than I ever was prior to my meeting him —and who makes it easier as time goes on to resist his offer as matchmaker.

2
Treacys in Killasmeestia

There were no Jews in or near Killasmeestia where I was born and raised, and few Protestants. It is a rural area in Laoighis County, Ireland, about 60 miles southwest of Dublin. Its principal landmark is the Catholic church.

A framed certificate in my study testifies to my receiving Communion for the first time on May 2, 1926 in this Gothic church. In the same church I was baptized on June 8, 1919, a few days after my birth, and in it on June 19, 1944 I celebrated Mass as a priest for the first time. Events in this little stone church built in the middle of the last century have been milestones in my life and the lives of my parents, a sister and two brothers. Around the church is a cemetery, "God's Acre", where my parents and paternal grandparents are buried.

Sunday morning in Killasmeestia still stands out clear in my mind as I look back over the years. There were few automobiles but in an area 98 percent Catholic, nearly everyone attended Sunday Mass. They traveled on foot, by bicycle or in horse or donkey-drawn carts. It was surprising how in a congregation of more than 300, one person could be missed. Failure to attend Sunday Mass usually meant illness and so gave concern to friends and neighbors. The great effort everyone made to attend Mass communicated to one young churchgoer the supreme importance of that hour with the priest on Sunday morning. While still in grade school I decided that to offer Mass for people would be the greatest service I could give them. It would mean, in the absence of a high school in the area, early leaving home and friends as part of a long climb to the priesthood, but the desire was so strong that I was prepared even at the age of 13 to make every sacrifice demanded.

From the age of three I was taken to Sunday Mass by my parents and I shall always be grateful to them and to the people of Killasmeestia who by example more than by words communicated their values to me. The Mass has undergone many external changes since my ordination in 1944 but the heart of it is the same. It is a faith encounter with God and while I have celebrated it in St. Peter's in Rome, in Jerusalem and Bethlehem, I find a special joy in celebrating it in Killasmeestia where I first assisted at Mass as a small boy with my parents and where I witnessed the faith of a community sharing this encounter with me Sunday after Sunday. I saw the Mass adding joy to life at weddings, comfort in sorrow at funerals and truly mattering in the lives of these people and in mine.

Formal religious education was given in the local public school which I attended. We had two public schools in the area, one for Protestants and one for Catholics, though out of a student body of a hundred in the school I attended there were at least 15 Protestants. The Government required five hours of instruction in secular subjects every day. The local pastor, Catholic or Protestant, served as manager and the principal and teachers were free to give religious instruction after the secular requirement was met. In our school the Protestants were excused from religion classes but they played in the school yard until we were finished so that we could all go home together. I was never conscious of any religious bigotry among neighbors in that part of Ireland or any attempt to convert a Protestant.

Long before I knew what the ecumenical movement stood for, I lived it and saw it lived in Tid Nolan's house. Tid was unmarried and she lived in a small two-room thatched house adjacent to the church and school which she shared with a bachelor brother. At noon recess from school her kitchen was filled with grade school students, eating lunch by her fire, drinking tea, seeking consolation from the frustrations of school. John Roe or George Moynihan, Protestants, were as welcome as Joe O'Connor or William Treacy to the comfort around Tid's fire as with motherly concern she would take a spoon and taste a cup of tea for one, add sugar to the cocoa of another, always adding a word of encouragement to the young who were finding the road to knowledge a difficult boreen (road) to travel.

We received a good foundation for our beliefs in school but I can see the greater unspoken influence of the community. Theological commentaries might be written on a phrase frequently on the lips of people as they accepted death, suffering, separation: "Welcome to the will of God". How is God present in the world He created? How is He present to a grieving widow and family? My contemporaries were aware of God's presence in their everyday lives, in sorrow and in joy, without being able to define it.

On more than one occasion I witnessed the spirit of community when neighbors carried the body of one who had died to the church and opened and closed the grave. The cross is a mystery that is a challenge to Christians throughout life. I remember the challenge it was to me as a boy of seven attending an interment in the local cemetery. I knew the neighbor who had died and the neighbors who closed the grave. They never spoke to me about faith in the Risen Jesus and the mystery of His love sealed by His death on the cross that is at the heart of the Christian message. But when they had covered the grave and put their clay-covered shovels on top of the fresh red earth in the form of a cross, I glimpsed the hope and struggle that this gesture was meant to express.

The grade school I attended was a simple three-room building erected in 1886. It did not boast of running water, electric light, a library or central heating. What heat we had depended on contributions of firewood from parents of students as the new Irish Government, which took the helm of Irish affairs in 1922 after eight centuries of British rule, evidently was unable to budget for such items. The situation in regard to high school education was even more appalling. There was no high school within 20 miles of our area and those that existed farther away were religious schools with high tuition rates. Only about half a dozen of the hundred enrolled in Killasmeestia school when I was there succeeded in getting a high school education, possible only because their parents were able to pay the fees required of boarders in a private school. My parents had worked hard acquiring and working their land and could afford to have me go to St. Kieran's School some 30 miles away in the city of Kilkenny. It was staffed for the most part by priests. High school in Ireland was a five-year course at the end of which we took a government examination that qualified us for entry into the university or a seminary.

St. Kieran's reflected the mood of the times. It provided a needed service and yet was woefully lacking in what we most needed as young boys away from the warmth of home. There was little interest in students except in regard to our academic performance; but if we were guilty of infractions of its many rules, then we received attention from professor to dean and perhaps all the way to the president. I suffered a great deal at St. Kieran's from loneliness.

During these years the longing to be a priest and to celebrate Mass grew, though few of the priests who dealt with me in the classroom did anything to inspire a love of the priesthood in me. They were teachers, following for the most part a philosophy expressed by their senior member, Father Frank Lawlor. Frequently and in good faith he would say, "There is only one good argument to get a student to learn—that is a cane."

I am sure that many of the priest-professors were frustrated by their classroom assignments. They probably had sought the priesthood as I was to do, dreaming of an assignment to a country parish to minister to the people in a variety of ways, and their academic ability led a bishop to assign them to a classroom. Because of the suffering I experienced at St. Kieran's, I determined that when I was a priest I would build no walls between myself and others—I would know them, not just academically or as parishioners but as persons.

In June 1937 I prepared to take the Leaving Certificate Examination set by the government and to go on to prepare for the priesthood. There were various seminaries to which aspirants to the priesthood could go—in Ireland, Paris, Rome, Louvain in Belgium. Because my vision of the priesthood was as I saw it exercised in Killasmeestia, I applied for acceptance by my local bishop, Dr. Patrick Collier, a severe and stern taskmaster. I was accepted and given a scholarship to the National Seminary, St. Patrick's, Maynooth, outside Dublin to prepare myself to be a priest in my native Ireland, close to my parents, my brothers and sister and the people I loved.

My parents did not push me into the decision but when I told them that summer night in 1937 of my acceptance by the seminary, two words said with feeling spoke volumes. Both said, "Thank God."

3
Maynooth—Seminary Days

In September 1937, I joined 75 freshmen from all over Ireland at St. Patrick's Seminary, Maynooth, for a course that would cover three years of study in Arts and Philosophy leading to a university degree, and four years of Scripture, Church History and Theology. About half of the 75 went on to be ordained.

This seminary has an interesting background. In 18th Century Ireland, the British Penal Laws had proscribed the Catholic Faith. Priests were hunted and killed and to operate a seminary would have been a capital offense. Young men managed to get to Rome, Paris or Spain to study for the priesthood and returned in various disguises to carry on an underground ministry. The British Government was aware of this but unable to stop it and found the political views of the European-trained priests, especially those from France, to be particularly distasteful.

A bold plan was presented by the Government to the Irish bishops: to build a native seminary where Irishmen could study for the priesthood in their own country. It would be subsidized by Britain in return for which the Irish bishops granted concessions to England. The principal concession was the right of Britain to veto the appointment of certain clergymen as bishops in Ireland. Anxious to have a seminary, the Irish bishops agreed. In 1796, 40 students and five professors took possession of Stoyte House, the residence of the chief steward on the estate of the Duke of Leinster, some 15 miles northwest of Dublin. This was the nucleus of what was to become the largest seminary in the world with an average enrollment of 600.

Freshmen at Maynooth were called "chubs." One alumnus describes the freshman experience: "One can see the self-conscious airs of that time, and the faces grave beyond the years. With the wind filling our sails we seemed to be setting out into the seas of knowledge to their faraway dim horizons. What matter if our ships were frailer than we deemed and have never voyaged to the end of our dreams."

Maynooth to London is less than an hour away by jet plane today, but it was centuries away from a young "chub" beginning his preparation for the priesthood in his native Ireland and a distinguished American rabbi at a London synagogue. But God had plans for a bridge between this London rabbi and the Irish Roman Catholic clerical student that neither dreamed of in 1937.

Maynooth gave me rich educational and spiritual opportunities. To live with 600 young men, gathered from the four corners of Ireland and animated by the same ideals, was a support of incalculable value. The human wealth of a society of young men formed around the altar of Maynooth chapel, looking forward to service together to God's people in our native land, stimulated personal growth and love. But otherwise life on the windswept plain of Maynooth was austere, as was the theological fare in the classroom. The never-failing good humor of classmates, their resilience and warm comradeship made up for many deficiencies, not the least of which was the ignoring of emotional and cultural needs.

Studies, discipline, the challenges of the seminary generally, were all conditions I accepted without too much pain and effort on my road to the priesthood. Returning home to the farm for a long summer, away from congenial companions and the spiritual support they gave, was a much more difficult challenge. And so in the summer of 1939 as war clouds formed on the horizon, I found myself studying the billboards that attracted young men to military service. Most of them showed an aviator looking at a plane against the sky and the words, "The thrill of sky and sea can be yours—join the Royal Air Force." Several times that summer I almost gave up the intention of returning to the seminary as I contemplated impending war and four more long summers between myself and the goal that meant much to me. But I did return that September of 1939, soon after England had declared war on Germany. The following June, as a defeated English army was retreating at Dunkirk, I took the examination for a B.A. degree in Classics and Philosophy. The priesthood seemed much closer the following September as I began the study of Theology.

At the end of my third year of Theology, I was ordained a subdeacon, which meant that at the age of 24 I pledged myself in total service outside marriage to my Church. Vocations to the priesthood were plentiful in Ireland and at times priests were encouraged to serve overseas and return to Ireland when needed. One evening the dean made a special announcement to those being ordained the following June who would not be needed for a few years in an Irish diocese. Volunteers were being requested by a bishop on the West Coast of America, in a place called Seattle. One of my classmates in Kilkenny and my roommate for four years in Maynooth, William Meany, had two uncles in Seattle with whom he corresponded. He encouraged me to volunteer even if he could not because of a teaching assignment; I did, and the necessary permission from my bishop was obtained and plans were made to get transportation in wartime.

Meanwhile the studies continued. There were no more summer vacations in the way. We rehearsed for our first Mass and the administration of the Sacraments. We preached and studied and prayed and finally on a clear, beautiful, sunny June 18, 1944, we filed two-by-two into the magnificent Maynooth chapel to have Archbishop John McQuaid of Dublin impose hands on us and commission us "to celebrate Mass, to offer sacrifice for the living and the dead . . . to preach, to bless, to sanctify human life and its strivings." This was priesthood—this was the vision dimly seen by a country boy in Killasmeestia. Through the years it had been pondered, prayed about, agonizingly appraised and pursued, now to become a reality.

I believe each of us must experience the Exodus. We must experience our own weakness and inability to cope with the problems and pain of life, as the Israelites did in Egypt, and then discover that through God we are freed from the slavery of our individual fears. Much as I wanted to be a priest, I was often discouraged on my way toward that goal. I felt the strain of the long, lonely summers when I was neither "fish nor fowl," neither fully accepted as a lay person nor as belonging in clerical company. I knew times of anxiety about my health when one bout of pleurisy kept me in the hospital for many months and under observation for tuberculosis. There were hidden fears known to God alone. Now as I walked down the aisle of the college chapel, I realized the fears were all gone. God had called me to be His ambassador among men. I was a priest—forever. He had assured me of His love and the only reaction was tears. I wonder if the Israelites did not have a good cry sometime after they crossed the Red Sea and realized their deliverance. I must talk to the Rabbi about this.

4
Maynooth and its Unopened Windows

Like any other Catholic seminary of its time, Maynooth presented the seminarian with a triumphalistic view of the Church as possessing all the treasures of wisdom and knowledge. The seminary system as we knew it saw all too little to recommend outside the Church. But history offers some explanation in the case of Ireland. Less than a century before I entered Maynooth, Ireland suffered one of its greatest national disasters when the potato crop failed in 1846, 1847 and 1848. This was the staple food of the majority of the eight million peasants living on small holdings as sharecroppers. Emigration and starvation accounted for the loss of four million people as a result of that famine. Such was the absence of the ecumenical spirit that in parts of Ireland, starving Catholics were given soup if they renounced their faith and joined the Protestant Church. I have heard the word "souper" applied to a person who would compromise his principles. A people who had suffered so much for loyalty to their faith could be understandably suspicious in regard to dialogue with non-Catholics.

Each September Maynooth took the starry-eyed 18-year-olds from the high schools of Ireland, aspirants to the priesthood, and for a period of seven years taught them to be excellent "maintenance" men for a system that was not to be tampered with or changed in any way.

We were governed by the "Rule", a long list of seminary regulations for every hour of the day. Where the seminary rule left off, Canon Law took over, and any remaining hole in the dike was filled by the "Maynooth Statutes", a body of legislation drawn up by the Irish bishops which regulated clerical dress, prayer, entertainment, recreation, relationships. The worst sin

17

for the Maynooth man was "singularity", a uniqueness in dress, views or style of life. Everyone was expected to conform. Rubrics governed how you held your eyes during services ("downcast"), how you stood ("erect" or "bowed"), when to stand and when to kneel. It was easy to forget the purpose of the service as you became engrossed in the externals. We did not read newspapers, nor was contact with the world outside our walls encouraged.

There was a Protestant church at the college gate, but it would have been regarded as high treason to attend a Sunday service in it. We were victims of the sad split among Christians at the time of Luther which led to persecution of brother by brother, of war and enmities which still engulf parts of Ireland. And in Maynooth, contact with members of the Jewish faith was non-existent, a situation which had not been remedied in my life during the years prior to 1960 when I met Rabbi Levine.

Such was the background of the priest who stepped into the office of the Rabbi in 1960 and announced he was the Catholic representative appointed by Archbishop Thomas Connolly to the interfaith panel being assembled by the Rabbi for a weekly television program that came to be called CHALLENGE.

I had been formed and fashioned to be loyal to my Church and its views, whatever my personal feelings. I was suspicious of the stranger, hesitant and afraid to put forth an individual viewpoint that was not "official". This accounted for the many quotations I used in the first years of the program. Maynooth taught me to be a "safe" man. CHALLENGE forced me to grow into my true Christian self.

By his patience and love the good Rabbi undid many of the negative influences and strengthened many of the positive influences of my seminary training. By being responsible for my television appearances each Sunday night with himself and a

Protestant minister, he exposed me to the great insights of Judaism which helped me to understand my Christian faith more fully. Through dialogue with my Protestant colleague I realized the truth of something which had remained hidden from me in Maynooth, that what united me to my Protestant brothers was more important than what divided us.

Frequently the Rabbi shocked my Maynooth-formed outlook by his statements. Brotherhood appeared to be the sum total of his religion. He saw all men as brothers and seemed rather casual about boundaries for men in their relationship to God. This was not easy to accept for me—formed to think very much about the Church as a society of believers with very definite qualifications for membership. De facto the Rabbi was preparing me to understand the new clarifications of Catholic doctrine coming from Vatican Council II. In one of the documents, "The Pastoral Constitution on the Church in the Modern World", I found echoes of many of his statements:

> "A new humanism is emerging in the world, a humanism in which man is primarily defined by his responsibility toward his brother and toward history."

Maynooth raised me with a great distrust of myself as well as of others because of the emphasis in theology on the weakness of human nature. Today I happily hear our leading theologians in Maynooth and elsewhere telling us that the human heart tends to expand rather than to shrivel when an atmosphere of trust and support is provided, and they have incorporated this philosophy into seminary training.

In September 1972 I was again in Dublin, thinking over the past, thinking over Maynooth and its role in my life. I thought of the years since I left Maynooth and of my friendship with Rabbi Levine and so many fine Jewish people in Seattle. The thought came to me that I had never been to a synagogue in Ireland or met any Irish Jews. I ascertained that Orthodox services would be held at 9 a.m. that day in the Adelaide Road Synagogue, one of the oldest in Ireland, and decided to attend.

I was present for the entire service and joined the congregation in the hall afterwards for their social hour or *kiddush cup*. It was the Feast of Tabernacles, the Feast of the Ingathering of the Harvest. It was a special harvest feast for me, a celebration of a new understanding of priesthood filled with love for the Jewish people; I was pleased and happy to be united with them as brothers and fellow countrymen in the worship of our common Father. It was a harvest festival made possible by the influence of men like Rabbi Levine and Pope John who opened windows for me that had been left unopened in Maynooth, as indeed they had been throughout the entire Catholic Church.

In our seminary days we were often taken for granted and often took each other for granted. This is to lose the sense of wonder, the sense of mystery that is in every life. People need people, priests need priests, to keep this sense of wonder, of mystery in life; the priest is, after all, a minister of Him "Whose glory the heavens and the earth show forth". In Maynooth I met some of the finest people it could be any man's good fortune to meet along the road of life. But its austere training ignored emotional and cultural needs and left me hesitant, for example, to express appreciation or a "well done" to a brother priest for some accomplishment. In *My New Curate*, Canon Sheehan, an alumnus of Maynooth, tells of a young priest who had been called to preach in the presence of the bishop. Discouraged and depressed, he came home and told his elderly pastor about the experience. The wise old priest analyzed the situation:

. . . when Father Lethaby called the next day he looked depressed and gloomy enough.

"Well," I said, "a great success, of course?"

"I'm afraid not," he said moodily.

"You broke down badly just in the middle?"

"Well, no, indeed; there was certainly no breakdown, but the whole thing was evidently a failure."

"Let me see," I cried. "There are certain infallible indications of the success or failure of a sermon. Were there any priests present?"

"About 20, I think," he replied. "That was the worst of it. You don't mind people at all."

"And weren't they very enthusiastic," I asked, "when you returned to the sacristy?"

"No, indeed. Rather the contrary, which makes me think that I said something either perilous or ill-advised."

"Humph! Didn't any fellow come up to you and knock the breath out of your body by slapping you on the back?"

"No!" he replied sadly.

"Didn't any fellow say: *Prospere procede, et regna?*" (Proceed prosperously and reign!)

"No!" he said. "It was just the other way."

"Didn't any fellow shake you by the hand even, and say: Prosit! prosit!! prosit!!!'" (To your health!)

"I'm afraid not," he said gloomily.

"That's bad. Not even *macte virtute esto, Titus Manlius?*" (Be of good courage).

"No," he said. "There was no indication of sympathy whatsoever."

"Didn't any fellow drop into the vernacular, and say: 'Put the hand there. Sure I never doubted you,' and wring your hand as if he wanted to dislocate it?"

"No, no, no! There was simply dead silence."

"And perhaps they looked at you over their shoulders, and whispered together, as they put their surplices into their bags, and stared at you as if you were a sea-monster?"

"Something that way, indeed," said the poor curate.

"Did the bishop make any remark?"

"Yes. The bishop came over and said that he was very grateful, indeed, for that beautiful sermon. But that, of course, was purely conventional."

"And the people? How did they take it?"

"They were very quiet and attentive, indeed: apparently an intelligent congregation."

"You don't think you were talking over their heads?"

"No, indeed. Even the poor women who were gathered under the pulpit stared at me unmercifully; and I think a few persons were much affected."

I waited a few minutes to draw my deductions. But they were logical enough.

"My dear boy," I said at length, "from a long and profound experience of that wilful thing called human nature, allow me to tell you that every indication that you have mentioned points to the fact that you have preached not only an edifying and useful, but a remarkable sermon—"

"Oh, that's only your usual goodness, Father Dan," he broke in. "I'm quite certain it was a failure. Look at the attitude of the priests!"

"That is just my strongest foundation," I replied. "If their enthusiasm had taken the other shapes I suggested, I should have despaired."

5
Beginnings in the Priesthood

I remember Rabbi Levine telling me how he had returned to Duluth for summer vacation a year before his ordination and while there was asked to preach at the Yom Kippur Eve service in the synagogue attended by his family. This is a lengthy service on the holiest day in the Jewish calendar. Standing at the side of the Ark, out of respect even though he could have been seated, was his aged father. It was a time of fulfillment for this devout immigrant family. At the end of the long service, overcome with emotion, Mr. Levine collapsed and died—early on Yom Kippur day, which for a Jew, Rabbi told me, was a blessed way to die.

I can understand the sentiments of the Levine family at the Yom Kippur service that night as I recall my own family and friends gathered around the altar in Killasmeestia on June 19, 1944 when I celebrated my first Mass. From earliest childhood I had seen the awe and reverence on the faces of grown-ups in this church when a priest took bread and wine as Jesus did at the Passover meal His last night on earth, and did what Jesus commanded be done in memory of Him. They believed that in response to the words of Jesus repeated by the priest over the elements of bread and wine, "This is my body . . . This is my blood", Jesus once again became present in a special way to men. In Gaelic speaking areas of Ireland the people were especially enthusiastic about expressing their faith in the Mass and at the consecration would sing out, "Cead mile failte", the traditional greeting to a guest coming to the home, "a hundred thousand welcomes". Now I was standing at the altar and seeing the same faith, the same reverence on the faces of these friends and neighbors that I had seen as a child. In their reverent acceptance of the consecrated bread from this priest of one day, they assured me that, though one of them, I was now called from among them and ordained to serve them and God in a special way.

As I cycled to the church that morning I paused near a field purchased many years earlier by my father. According to a tradition, a priest on the run celebrated Mass in a glen near there during the 18th century when there was a price on every priest's head. I paused to salute these brave ancestors who loved the Mass so much that they risked their lives to be present at it. I resolved that morning before celebrating my first Mass that I would endeavor to keep my reverence for the Mass always, not to let routine dim its splendor. Thank God, each day since has seen the reverence deepen and the sense of its splendor increase.

I was assigned as a curate to a small country church about 40 miles from my home in a place called Ballycallan, Kilkenny. On Sunday I would travel five to ten miles on a bicycle, commuting between two churches. The months went by quickly for a happy young priest who shared a residence with a congenial fellow curate by the name of Father James Walsh. But Christmas came and plans for my travels to Seattle were nearing completion.

In February I set out for England with three suitcases, one containing books; another, clothes; the third, passports, tickets and personal data. A well-meaning priest but one not too well informed about war-time London told me that if I had difficulty getting a hotel in London, to seek help from friends of his at a convent in Hammersmith, "a small place outside London". I had visions of a small country village, and so finding it impossible to get a hotel room in London in February 1945, I set out by subway for Hammersmith. It was the end of a long day that saw me leave Dublin by boat at 8 a.m., reach Holyhead, Wales, at noon and take a train from there to London.

Carrying three suitcases during rush hour on a subway is a day's work in itself. I had to change trains at King's Cross and laid the suitcases side-by-side on the platform. It seemed the battle was over and that Hammersmith, that "small place outside London", was just around the corner. So I relaxed. The train came in and I put two suitcases on it next to the door, the ones containing clothes, passport, tickets. Just as I turned to get the third one on the platform, the train pulled away. I was momentarily stunned and then ran to find some official to help. When I found one he asked the number of the train. I hadn't the slightest idea. Then in a fatherly voice he said, "Look, son, there is no guard on the train. Your luggage is close to the door. The train was crowded. Someone must have noticed what happened and will calmly walk off with your suitcases."

Recalling the words of Bishop Collier that if I did not sail for America early in the new year, he was sending me to Hexham and Newcastle in England, I figured that by losing my ticket and travel documents, I had lost my chance for Seattle. It was 10 p.m. After much pleading, the elderly dispatcher said he would make "some inquiries", not to expect any results but to come back after midnight.

I returned at midnight and a young woman was in charge. She looked at me and said, "You won't believe it—but my boss was telling me about you after I came on duty and how you expected to find your luggage. Honestly, I laughed. Then I went out on the platform as a train pulled in. The doors opened and I saw two suitcases. I barely had time to check the name. But here they are, untouched." And so the possibility of reaching Seattle was real again after a nightmarish two hours in war-torn London.

At Hammersmith I went to the nearest police station to get help in finding a hotel room. The desk sergeant had no success.

Exhausted but at peace, I sat down in a chair and fell asleep. Later the sergeant came over and asked if I would like to lie down. As he led me down a jail corridor he apologized for the accommodations. He gave me a single blanket and a cell in solitary confinement. The next morning I slipped into line with the prisoners to wash up and then the officer of the day "released" me and I was on my way for my rendezvous with the troopship—and eventually with Rabbi Levine.

I sailed from Grenock, Scotland. For ten days the Ile de France, serving as a troopship with a British crew, zigzagged across the Atlantic to avoid submarines and on February 25, 1945 I stood on her deck with G.I.'s—tears streaming down their faces—looking at the Statue of Liberty that many of them thought they would never see again as they fought in North Africa, Sicily and Normandy for the ideals it represented. It was a welcome to America with its bravest that I shall never forget.

St. Alphonsus parish in Seattle to which I was assigned was typical of the many parishes in the United States that had sent a large number of its young men to war. There was restrained rejoicing in May 1945 when the war in Europe ended. But then we began to read the full story of Nazi tyranny, especially in regard to Jews who once again had been led as Isaiah said "like sheep to the slaughter" to the gas chambers of concentration camps. The stories shocked the world; they moved me to compassion for the Jewish people and strengthened a desire to draw close to them.

In the summer of 1946 when I was transferred to St. James Cathedral, I found a pastor who delegated authority easily, the late Monsignor John Gallagher, and five other young priests with whom I spent three of the happiest years of my priesthood. There was such camaraderie among us that though each of us was entitled to a full day off each week, we would frequently come back for the evening meal to enjoy the banter and good humor of a happy family around the table.

Then one evening in September 1947, the pastor called me to his study. In the next block to the Cathedral was the chancery, the office of the archbishop. The chancellor was then ill and I was asked to go over to the chancery for a few weeks to help him out. I knew nothing about chancery work as Irish bishops did not have such elaborate administrative machinery and most of the priests assigned to chancery work in the U.S. had post-graduate training in Canon Law which I did not have. The "few weeks" lengthened into 16 years.

From boyhood I had had an attraction for pastoral work and even though the 16 years in the chancery were extremely busy, they were in a sense years of waiting. We wait for much in life —for growth, for understanding, for the outcome of decisions, for those conjunctions of time and place and persons that mark the milestones in our lives. I was to learn much more of waiting in the years to come, of its discipline and of the sustained expectancy which is hope.

When I arrived in Seattle I was determined to be loyal to my commitment to my bishop in Ireland and much as I loved the Pacific Northwest, I kept myself psychologically ready to leave for Ireland. One day soon after I began work in the chancery, Bishop Gerald Shaughnessy called me to his office and asked if I would like to transfer from Ireland to Seattle. I told him yes, if my bishop in Ireland was willing to release me. He said he would begin negotiations but would make it clear that he had taken the initiative in the matter. Within a few days, Bishop Shaughnessy suffered a stroke and the priest who was his secretary told me to wait for action until a new bishop came.

Bishop Connolly, who arrived in 1948, was anxious to get other Irish priests and did not want to give the impression in

Ireland that he held on to those sent on a temporary basis. He asked me to wait for a few years before taking final action on the transfer. Meanwhile my bishop in Ireland was becoming impatient with the delay and expressed a strong wish, but no command, that I return. After four years of waiting, he gave permission in June 1951 for me to remain permanently in Seattle.

From 1947 to 1963 I was secretary on the marriage tribunal which handles all Church legal matters in regard to marriage. Frequently the witnesses needed in a case in Seattle lived in Florida or Maine and witnesses needed in New York or Texas lived in Seattle. A great deal of time was spent routing requests for testimony to other dioceses and writing and processing similar requests for the testimony of witnesses living in the Seattle area. I was always at heart a rebel against these procedures which are now being corrected and my frustrations found outlets in various forms. To help couples achieve a lasting and happy marriage, I organized marriage preparation courses and invited leading psychologists, lawyers, judges, doctors, married couples and divorced persons to share their insights with those contemplating marriage and to point out possible pitfalls in the road ahead.

Many calls of a pastoral nature came to me at the Cathedral and later at the Church of the Immaculate after I went there in 1949. One resulted in my working for ten years on the Seattle-King County Commission on Alcoholism. I had been celebrating Mass regularly at the county jail and was served breakfast one morning by a trustee in spotless white uniform. A few mornings later I found this same man, drunk, tattered and dirty on the rectory doorstep. He was one of the hundreds of victims of alcoholism living on Skid Road in Seattle, arrested so often that they spent much of their lives in jail. I had traveled through Skid Road hundreds of times, seeing but not heeding, and then

Skid Road was dropped on my doorstep in the person of this derelict member of the human family. Many times, too, I had read Jesus' admonition to go first and be reconciled with my brother and then come and offer my gifts at the altar and had not understood that I needed to be reconciled with my Skid Road brother.

This man and others like the destitute old man dying in King County Hospital taught me early in my priesthood that ministering to others is not a one-way street. I was called one night to the bedside of an old man whose name I never knew. It was a warm night and he complained that he could not breathe. He was in such distress that talking with him, reading to him or trying to pray with him were out of the question and so I picked up an old newspaper and began to fan him—my suffering brother whom I had not met before that night. For two or three hours I fanned him and when he became drowsy, I prepared to leave. "I have had a few friends during my life," he said, "but no one has ever done more for me than you did tonight." A man in need, a cast-off newspaper, a simple effort, a caring presence, an acceptance—these constituted the great gift in this man's life. And ever since he has been giving to me for he keeps before me the essence of giving, the utter simplicity of a gift, the bared, uncluttered relationship of brother to brother.

It is easy to grow tired of waiting, to drop out from school, from marriage, from caring for others, from the priesthood. I thank God that I waited for two bishops to make up their minds about what country I would serve in, for Pope John to throw open windows long closed, for the opportunity to join Rabbi Levine on CHALLENGE.

6
Here Comes the Rabbi

During my first years in Seattle I had often read newspaper items about the Senior Rabbi of Temple De Hirsch and I admired his wisdom and leadership. Never for a moment did I consider myself in his league. One morning in the spring of 1960 as I walked past the Archbishop's office in the chancery, the door opened and he came out with a distinguished looking gentleman beside him. He beckoned me to the door of his office and said, "Father Treacy, I would like to introduce you to Rabbi Levine". We shook hands and parted but the memory of that meeting is deeply etched on my mind. Archbishop Connolly, with his usual reticence, did not disclose that he was considering a partnership between the Rabbi and myself.

I went back to my work filing papers and checking marriage documents. A month or so after the encounter, the Archbishop called me into his office and told me that Rabbi Levine had approached him about a television program involving a priest, a minister and a rabbi to discuss religious freedom, church and state relations, religious prejudice and similar topics coming to the fore with John F. Kennedy's campaign for president. He was not overly optimistic about its long-range success but wanted me to represent the Catholic viewpoint and to work out the details with the Rabbi. I was honored but awed by the proposal. Except for the brief greeting outside the Archbishop's office, I had never met a rabbi but I dialed the number of Temple De Hirsch and made an appointment with Rabbi Levine.

I had never been to a synagogue before, but something within me drew me to the Jewish people, an admiration for their faith and constancy, a sympathy for their suffering through the centuries. I was thrilled and shy about meeting the Rabbi. He was gracious to me and enthusiastic about the proposed program as an instrument to lessen religious prejudice in the Northwest. Later I learned that his initial reaction to the Catholic representative was one of keen disappointment but it is his prerogative to relate it.

He asked me if I had any suggestions for the Protestant member of the panel. While I knew many Protestants from my work as director of the Religious Information Program, my contact with ministers of other faiths was very limited. I confessed as much to the Rabbi. Then he suggested Dr. Martin Goslin, pastor of Plymouth Congregational Church, as one who had experience on television and a "feel" for what he had in mind. Our first project together was to call on Dr. Goslin at his residence and explain—mostly in the words of the Rabbi—the proposed program. He readily agreed to participate. The three of us went to see William Warren, president of station KOMO. This quiet, kindly man of few words assured us that the station wanted our program to succeed in promoting better understanding in our community and in lessening prejudice and ill will and would give us prime time. He was the one who suggested it be called CHALLENGE.

In September 1960 the first program went on the air, a discussion of religious freedom. I was scared of the Jewish and Protestant audiences—and also of the Catholic. It took many programs and many months before I found myself at ease with my two distinguished colleagues. My tendency was to sit back in admiration and just listen, forgetting that I was part of the team, too. My greatest difficulty was having no eyeball-to-eyeball contact with an audience and I shall always be grateful to Don McCune, our announcer, for remaining on the set as my audience during the first tapings. With one interested looking spectator, I was encouraged to proceed. Then the unseen audience began to talk back through letters and calls and I began to feel their presence at the tapings.

Rabbi has often said that this program would not have been possible had it not been for Pope John XXIII. Through Vatican Council II and his own saintly personality, his love for people, his warm empathy, he opened windows through which Catholics could look with greater sensitivity and understanding to people of other faiths. His great spirit permeated the Council and his influence spread throughout the world. Both Rabbi and I feel it was largely Pope John's example and his great spirit and desire for reconciliation that provided the climate for CHALLENGE.

CHALLENGE owes a great deal, too, to Dr. Goslin, a man of great learning and openness, for he helped to form the traditions that marked the program from its beginnings. He and Rabbi Levine came into my life at a most opportune time. Experiences during my first 41 years, confirmed by Vatican Council II, had shown me possibilities for reconciliation; now I was ready to join others in working actively toward it.

Rabbi means teacher. I have learned more about life and about God from this teacher than from any other I have ever had, even in the seminary. With my traditionalist Catholic training, I was reluctant to believe that apart from creating a climate of respect and understanding, I would ever find great spiritual sharing with the Rabbi. I found him to be real, to be honest, to be himself. While Reform Judaism meant loyalty to certain basic principles of Judaism, I found that it left the Rabbi free to do his own interpreting without having to submit very frequently, if at all, to higher governing authorities. I was trained to subordinate my thinking to that of the Church. A principle of my training might be expressed: "Rome has spoken; the issue, therefore, has been resolved". This did not mean that it had been clarified or that I fully understood the positions taken by the Church, but I accepted them.

Frequently I found myself struggling with the Rabbi about fundamental Christian truths and seeking to formulate them to him, not in the scholastic language in which they were taught to me, but in biblical terms such as was happening at the Council. I had heard the statement of Pius XI about Catholics: "Spiritually we are Semites". I began to feel this strongly as the Rabbi opened up new insights about man's relationship to God and helped me to clarify my own notion of God.

Because of my friendship with Rabbi Levine I have learned that in my study of history certain pages were missing. The Crusades, for example, were presented as a Christian response to the plea of the Pope to free the Holy Places from Moslem rule and to make it possible for Christians to visit these places in freedom and safety. I did not know that the first Crusade began with a most un-Christian, inhuman gesture—the slaughter of thousands of Jews in the Rhineland. In fact, I learned that Jews were far from enthusiastic when they heard that Christians were going to have an ecumenical council. Because of the anti-Jewish legislation that unfortunately emanated from previous councils, Jewish communities frequently proclaimed a fast prior to such a council to seek God's protection for themselves.

Having learned some of these unsettling facts while Vatican Council was meeting between 1962 and 1965, I rejoiced at the invitation from Rabbi Levine to address his congregation and to join him in leading Christians and Jews in new directions together. Jews rejoiced at the prospect of better relations and I was received warmly as an ambassador of their much loved and admired Pope John. I believe they loved me as a spokesman for a Church that produced Pope John who greeted a Jewish delegation with "I am Joseph, your brother", a Pope who while on diplomatic service for the Church in Istanbul during World War II worked hard to obtain freedom for Jews fleeing Nazi tyranny.

To help Christians better understand our Jewish heritage, I arranged a Jewish Seder, the ceremonial Passover meal, for parishioners at St. Patrick's, Seattle, when I became pastor there in 1965, and invited Rabbi Levine and his cantor to help us understand the significance of that meal which is the basis for our Mass. We held this meal on Holy Thursday night, that year and in subsequent years, when according to Christian tradition Jesus observed it with His Apostles.

Collaboration and participation in Protestant services had also been frowned on by the Catholic Church because such contacts might lead to religious indifference, to a watering down of the Catholic faith. The Rabbi showed me the extent to which it was possible to participate in the religious service of another church without compromising one's own faith. He was invited to a camp for teenagers of the Baptist and Disciples of Christ Churches. His talks with the teenagers had touched their hearts and they invited him to their communion service and to receive communion with them. He gently declined, but added, "As you receive communion, which to you is the closest form of union with God, I will stand behind each one of you, conversing silently in prayer with God, and so He will come to us all in a special way at the same time".

It was in this same spirit that in 1965 when the new liturgical changes called for an altar facing the people that I asked Rabbi Levine to build one. He agreed immediately and his wife, Reeva, volunteered to do the art work on it. He knew how important the altar is in Catholic worship and he knew that I was not asking him to compromise his Jewish faith in making it. Today the altar is in St. Michael's Church, Olympia. Someday I hope it will find a place in an interfaith chapel at Camp

Brotherhood which we founded together in Northwest Washington.

Rabbi welcomed every opportunity to speak in Christian churches and before Christian groups. He had been active in the local chapter of the National Conference of Christians and Jews since coming to Seattle and so had many friends among Christians with whom he shared, as with me, not only theological insights but personal sorrows and joys.

In May 1962, year of the Seattle World's Fair, the Knights of Columbus invited me to a dinner to honor a mother singled out for special recognition. I had already been chaplain to the Knights and director of their religious advertising program for several years.

The invitation presented a problem for me as the time approached. Rabbi Levine wanted me to go out to dinner with him and Dr. Goslin to celebrate the end of our first year on television. I explained the other commitment and he assured me they would get me there on time. Then he said, "I have never attended a Knights of Columbus function. May I come to the dinner?" This appeal to my ecumenical conscience could not be refused and we proceeded to the Knights' dinner after our anniversary celebration.

There were the usual introductions before the Mother of the Year was escorted from an anteroom to the auditorium and as chaplain I was asked to address the guests. Then I sat down and the master of ceremonies began to read the citation: "Mary Delaney, born in Galmoy, County Kilkenny, in 1887, married John Treacy, 1918, blessed with four children. Her beloved spouse died March 1, 1948." All the facts were in order, but who provided them? And how touching to honor my 75-year-old mother in absentia. When the citation was finished, a band started to play outside the door of the auditorium. An honor guard entered to shouts and applause and then came my mother escorted by Archbishop Connolly. Rabbi Levine had been in on the secret from the beginning.

Newspapers carried a full account and a few days later I received a call from the World's Fair committee. My mother was to be "World's Fair Mother" and at noon on Mother's Day a chauffeured limousine took Mrs. Mary Treacy, who had never been outside her native Ireland before, and her son to the Space Needle for lunch with Fair committee members, Rabbi Levine and Dr. Goslin. Later that week she watched a taping of CHALLENGE.

Dr. Goslin left CHALLENGE and Seattle in 1962 to teach in a seminary and was succeeded on the program by Dr. Lynn Corson, senior pastor of University Methodist Church, who continued until his retirement in 1968. Dr. Corson's father and grandfather were Methodist ministers and he had had little contact with Catholics and Jews before becoming a CHALLENGE panelist. In 1968 on his farewell appearance for CHALLENGE, he spoke of what the program had done for him, confessing that as late as 1960 he had little of the spirit of CHALLENGE when he preached a "thundering sermon" on the danger to the republic of having a Catholic president.

In December 1973 Dr. Corson died suddenly of a heart attack while in Seattle on a visit from New Jersey. Four days earlier we had spent an afternoon together sharing our outlook on ministry, and it was exhilarating for me to learn how he had met recent challenges in his life and had grown so remarkably in wisdom and grace.

Rabbi and I preached at the memorial service for him in Seattle and it seemed eminently appropriate to me to offer as

Dr. Corson's farewell, one prayed by Pope John on the eve of his death:

Love one another, my dear children!
Seek rather what unites
Not what may separate you
From one another.
As I take leave, or better still,
As I say, "till we meet again",
Let me remind you of the
Most important things in life:
Our Blessed Saviour Jesus; His good news;
His Holy Church; truth and kindness . . .
I shall remember you all
And pray for you.

When Dr. Corson left CHALLENGE, Pastor Oscar Rolander of Our Redeemer's Lutheran Church joined us. He had been a missionary from 1947 to 1952 in Tanzania, East Africa, and has since returned to mission work. We still keep in close touch and with each communication my admiration for him grows. Early in our association I came to appreciate the great religious convictions that led both him and his wife, Doris, to serve in a remote area of Africa when he told me about the birth of his third child, a daughter. Because Doris had the negative RH blood factor, she was flown to Nairobi for the birth of their child. Communications were poor and Dr. Rolander did not hear for a month if she and the baby lived. I know the great love he and Doris had for one another; that month of waiting must have seemed years.

Dr. Rolander's place on CHALLENGE was taken by Dr. Robert Fine, pastor of Free Methodist Church, Seattle Pacific College. The soul of this great man was laid bare on CHAL-

LENGE one Sunday night as he shared with us his feelings soon after his vivacious 12-year-old daughter, Dolly, died on November 8, 1972. She came home from school the afternoon before with a severe headache and within a few hours died of an aneurism in the brain. In "Stand Up and Drink to God", a title he chose from a poem by G.K. Chesterton, Dr. Fine spoke of feeling like another Noah with grief sweeping over him like a deluge. It seemed to sweep everything from under him, and yet all the while there was the firm conviction that at the heart of the universe is goodness and love.

He recalled delightful ways Dolly remains with them and how friends of older children stayed with him and his wife, Betty, through the night after Dolly died and showed by their freedom and banter, their compassion and joy, how life goes on. He found tremendous strength in his faith and in the new insights that faith revealed to him at such a time, "especially the firm realization that what you have trusted in all along is reality".

CHALLENGE brought us all together—Protestant, Catholic, Jew—to discover initially how much we all had in common, but we came to share, too, a great deal more than a weekly half-hour on television. This led us to expect and to hope that the same thing was happening in the lives of our viewers. When CHALLENGE was discontinued in the fall of 1974, Don McCune confirmed this hope in a letter written on July 25, 1974:

Dear Father Treacy:

From now on you're on your own!

There won't be a "Black Lutheran" sitting in the corner waiting to spell out the subject and offering moral encouragement to a young Irish priest who dared to do what few people thought was possible . . . and in so doing . . . accomplished a quiet miracle in more lives than he could ever count if he lived to be a hundred!

You and the Rabbi . . . and all the others who came along to add their share over the years. All of the years of reaching out for gentleness and understanding . . . the lifting of stones which had laid unturned for centuries . . . letting in the light . . . proving that nothing is impossible for men of good faith.

And from one who was part of it . . . and who now walks away with a firmer step and a thankful heart . . . God Bless You, Father Treacy! May the wind be always at your back. May you continue to rise to the challenge and when your day is done may you reach the promised land before the Devil knows you're gone!

As ever,
Don

7
People-to-People

In the spring of 1963 Rabbi Levine decided to help implement a program suggested by President Eisenhower to bring people of different countries and cultures into friendly contact with each other. He gathered together representatives of various professions and religions and all set out under the leadership of the CHALLENGE panel—himself, Dr. Corson and me—for a two-month People-to-People tour of Europe and the Middle East.

Dr. Corson and I made a detour from Paris to visit the famous Protestant religious community at Taize, near the Swiss border. We flew to Lyons and stayed overnight with Dominican priests at their Latourette monastery near Lyons. It was the first time Dr. Corson had ever visited a Catholic monastery and months later I learned that I had taken a lot for granted. We talked with Father Jean Lintanf until midnight, bringing him greetings from an old friend in Seattle, Father Joseph Fulton, and then after showing me my room, he took Dr. Corson by the arm and escorted him to a room farther down the dimly lit corridor. Dr. Corson confessed later that another Dominican suddenly appeared from the pages of history, the infamous Torquemada, and as the corridor creaked he could hear the dread apparatus of the Inquisition at work.

The next day we drove to Taize and prayed together in the Church of Reconciliation. It was built by young Germans, both Catholic and Protestant, in reparation for the sins of their fathers. Prior to the building of the church, the monks, representing 17 different Protestant denominations, used the local Catholic church for worship with the blessing of Pope John, then Apostolic Nuncio to France. Roger Schutz, a Swiss Calvinist, founded the Taize community near the headquarters of

40

mediaeval monasticism in Cluny to provide a living witness to Christian unity. The community numbered 63 when we were there, with affiliated groups living and working in Algeria, Coventry, England, and the Gold Coast in Africa.

In Moscow I saw Rabbi swing into action and use every contact with people to foster unity, to break down a barrier. He came to me one evening and said he had met a black man in the Hotel Ukraine where we were staying, a Congolese diplomat who was a Catholic, and advised me to follow up on the contact. Next day I met Antoine Efformi, first secretary of the Congolese Embassy, in the dining room of the hotel and invited him and his wife to join me for dinner later in the week. I had been celebrating Mass while in Moscow in a small chapel in the apartment of the priest assigned to minister to American Embassy personnel. Each morning Marie Elizabeth Isaye, a young Belgian secretary to the Belgian ambassador, assisted at Mass and drove me back to the hotel. This was a time when the Congo was in turmoil following its newly declared independence from Belgium. I invited Marie Elizabeth to join me for dinner with Mr. and Mrs. Efformi and was startled by her vehement "No!" We talked for a while about People-to-People, about building bridges of understanding; for us this was living the Mass we had just shared. She agreed to come.

It was a very emotional evening for all of us and many tears were shed as we dined and drank some Georgian wine together. I learned that the attractive and talented Marie had spent some years as a social worker in the Congo and in the course of conversation found that Mrs. Efformi was from the town where Marie had worked. Memories flooded back as they talked. One that still touched her most, Marie said, was the response of the Moslem people in the small town in the Congo where she lived, to the news of her mother's death. Anxious to show their sympathy, they sent a delegation to the Catholic priest to request that a Mass be said for her and her mother. It was a beautiful sight later that evening to see this blond Belgian open the door of her sports car for the black Antoine and Mrs. Efformi from the Congo and drive them to their apartment.

During the tour I insisted on wearing clerical dress as a gesture, for what it was worth, of my faith in God. One day Dean John Leffler, former dean of St. Mark's Cathedral, Seattle, said to me, "You are an enigma to that Intourist guide". I suppose that after ten years in Komsomol, the Russian youth movement, and indoctrination in atheism, our official guide, Valentina Kotlaraskaya, must have had serious misgivings about religion and those who professed it. One day she approached me with, "I notice you do not come to breakfast. Where do you go in the mornings?" I usually had coffee with the priest in whose apartment I celebrated Mass. I told her this and then continued, "Valentina, in your book my values may be wrong. But you know that recently the daughter of Krushchev and her husband were received by Pope John." She smiled approvingly. "But they did not try to make Pope John a Communist and he did not try to make them Catholics. Let me be a priest and worship God in Moscow and I will respect your convictions."

Because of my interest in the ecumenical movement, I was anxious to visit Zagorsk, the famous Orthodox monastery about a hundred miles from Moscow. It could be reached only by car. Valentina was most helpful in arranging the visit, even to getting me a box lunch from the kitchen of the hotel. Accompanying me were Dean Leffler, Dr. Corson and Father George Hirschboeck of Maryknoll whom I had met in Moscow. Alexis, the aged Patriarch of the Russian Orthodox Church, was still alive and the head of the monastery was Archimandrite Pimen. He received us most graciously. He spoke some English

Father William Treacy, Sister Patricia Jacobsen and Rabbi Raphael Levine select pictures for *Wild Branch on the Olive Tree* as book nears completion.

(photo by Willard Hatch)

The Treacy home in Killasmeestia, County Laoighis, central Ireland, where Father Treacy grew up. Mixed farming was done on the land that surrounded it.

The Catholic church in Killasmeestia around which the life of the community revolved. Father Treacy's parents and paternal grandparents are buried in the churchyard cemetery.

An itinerant photographer stopped at Killasmeestia school in 1929. He photographed the four Treacy children: May, Joe, William and John.

Killasmeestia grade school. At the time Father Treacy attended the three-room school, there were about 100 students. There were two public schools in the area, one for Protestants and one for Catholics, though religious boundaries in this part of Ireland were not strictly kept and student bodies in both schools were mixed.

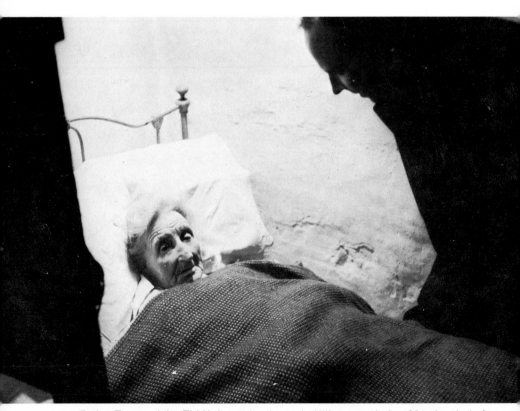

Father Treacy visits Tid Nolan at her home in Killasmeestia in 1961 shortly before her death. Tid lived next door to the grade school and welcomed the children who liked to eat their lunch at her hearth.

St. Kieran's College, Kilkenny, a boarding school for boys about 30 miles from Father Treacy's home.

Ordination Day, June 18, 1944, Maynooth. Father Treacy is flanked by his parents, younger brother, Joe, and sister, May, now Mrs. William Phelan.

Left: Father Treacy and his mother outside their home in 1935. Father, the eldest of four children, was then 16 years old and a boarder at St. Kieran's College, Kilkenny. Right: Father Treacy as a young curate at St. James Cathedral, Seattle.

Father Treacy with Maynooth classmates Father William Meany and Father Patrick J. Brophy in 1955 at a reunion in his mother's home in Killasmeestia.

Raphael Levine as a child of four with his parents and sister, Ida, in Vilna, Lithuania. Rabbi was the youngest of 12 children.

Left: Rabbi Levine's maternal grandfather known as "Lebel the Innkeeper" who died at the age of 104. Right: Rabbi's parents with one of their older sons.

Left: Raphael Levine as a student in Hebrew Union College, Cincinnati. He had already qualified as a teacher and as a lawyer before deciding to become a rabbi. Right: A rare time for relaxation while simultaneously a seminary student, a newspaper editor and leader of a student congregation in Indiana.

The first CHALLENGE panel on the television set, 1960: Father Treacy, Dr. Martin Goslin, Rabbi Levine.

The first CHALLENGE panel just after being presented a Special Award by the National Conference of Christians and Jews in 1962 for their contribution to greater understanding between religious groups. The program "Who Crucified Jesus?" was largely responsible for this award.

Dr. Lynn Corson, second Protestant panelist, Father Treacy and Rabbi Levine with long-time producer of CHALLENGE, Mrs. Marty Wilson, whose selection of topics and suggestions for approaching them helped to interest a large CHALLENGE audience every Sunday evening for 14 years. The program was unrehearsed and panelists did not discuss topics among themselves before the tapings.

The third CHALLENGE panel: Pastor Oscar Rolander, Father Treacy and Rabbi Levine. Pastor Rolander stayed with the program for two years until going to Geneva, Switzerland to direct mission work in Africa. Rabbi is seldom without the cane on which he carved some of his favorite quotations.

The authors with Ken Ritchey who directed CHALLENGE from its beginning until becoming producer two years before the regular series ended in the fall of 1974.

KOMO announcer Don McCune skillfully introduced and closed every CHALLENGE program for 14 years.

Dr. Robert Fine (center), pastor of Free Methodist Church, Seattle Pacific University, succeeded Dr. Rolander on the CHALLENGE panel and remained a member until the program ended. He was one of the leaders for the 1972 CHALLENGE tour to Israel and is seen here at the Kennedy Memorial near Jerusalem with Rabbi Moses Wyler, representing the Jewish National Fund, and Rabbi Levine.

William P. Woods, Chairman of the Board of Washington Natural Gas, presents Rabbi Levine with an award from the National Conference of Christians and Jews in 1971 in recognition of service to brotherhood.

In 1962 the Seattle Knights of Columbus surprised Father Treacy, then their chaplain, by naming his mother "Mother of the Year" and bringing her from Ireland to Seattle.

Mrs. Mary Treacy was also elected "World's Fair Mother" by the Seattle World's Fair Committee in 1962. Dr. Goslin and Rabbi and Reeva Levine join her and Father Treacy on a tour of the fairgrounds.

Every year since 1965 Father Treacy has arranged a Seder dinner for his parishioners at St. Patrick's, Seattle, and later St. Michael's, Olympia, on Holy Thursday evening. Here at St. Patrick's, Rabbi Levine conducted the ceremonial meal assisted by Leon Israel, Temple cantor.

Rabbi Levine, whose hobby is working with wood, made an altar for Father Treacy in 1965 when he was pastor of St. Patrick's Church, Seattle. Made of mahogany, birch and walnut, the altar was decorated with symbols designed by Mrs. Reeva Levine.

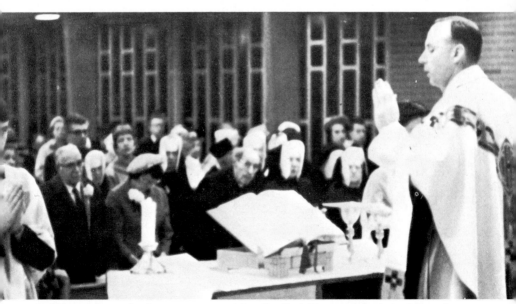

Rabbi and Reeva Levine were present for the first Mass celebrated at the altar Rabbi made in St. Patrick's Church, March 17, 1965. The altar is now in the baptistry of St. Michael's Church, Olympia.

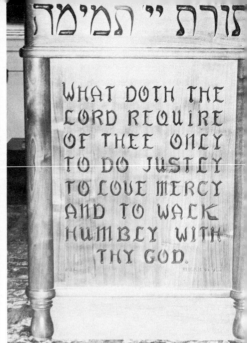

תורת יי תמימה

WHAT DOTH THE
LORD REQUIRE
OF THEE ONLY
TO DO JUSTLY
TO LOVE MERCY
AND TO WALK
HUMBLY WITH
THY GOD.

Left: Rabbi Levine at work in his basement shop. One of his "specialties" is tables with chessboard tops. He is seen here putting finishing touches on a chessboard figure. Right: A pulpit stand crafted and carved by Rabbi Levine. The quotation is from the prophet Micah, chapter 6.

A nest of five tables in colored mosaic depicting Judaism's symbols and ceremonial objects which took Rabbi 1000 hours of one year to make. The Torah is honored: "The Torah of God is perfect. It is a Tree of Life to them that hold fast to it." Symbols of the tribes of Israel and the chief holidays are alternated around the outer border.

Rabbi Iser Freund and Rabbi Levine initiated the first Jewish Youth Camp sponsored by the Western Association of Reform Rabbis which Rabbi Levine founded. The camp, held at Presbyterian Conference Grounds, Lake Tahoe, grew out of earlier experiences the two Rabbis had as counselors at Protestant camps. There are now nine regional Jewish youth camps throughout the country.

Rabbi Levine and a young camper at the first Jewish Youth Camp enjoy a game of chess.

The daily worship service at Lake Tahoe was held in the "Temple by the Lake", an improvised outdoor synagogue. The Torah for the Sabbath worship was lent by the Jewish community in Reno, Nevada.

More than 100 campers from the West Coast participated in the worship services at Lake Tahoe. The camp so appealed to Jewish youth that by the fourth year, quotas had to be set for participating congregations.

Rabbi, Friends View Site of Camp

Rabbi Raphael Levine, left, and friends viewed the Goldade farm, site of his proposed ecumenical camp near Mount Vernon. The others, from left, were Mrs. Levine, the Rev. William Treacy, Mrs. Leo Goldade and Mr. Goldade.

(*Times* staff photo by Ron DeRosa)

SEATTLE
Sunday Post-Intelligencer

L* SUNDAY, JANUARY 1, 1967 TWENTY CENTS

A Spiritual Oasis for the Skagit Vall

Rabbi Raphael Levine, right, showed Brotherhood farm site to Father William Treacy. Mt. Vernon area site was selected for Northwest ecumenical religious and brotherhood center.

Exterior of Fisher Lodge designed and constructed by students in the School of Architecture, University of Washington. On October 6, 1968, Governor Daniel Evans, honorary chairman of Camp Brotherhood, dedicated the lodge which has brought together 40,000 campers since its dedication.

Campers stroll near the pavilion, built in 1973, which now serves as a multi-purpose center.

Left: Rabbi Levine and Leo Levy in last-minute work on the Jewish retreat center in order to have it ready for formal opening in 1972. Temple De Hirsch Sinai sponsored the project and also built a small house for the chaplain. Right: Rabbi Levine with Wally Fisher at the naming of Fisher Lodge. The Fisher family have been outstanding benefactors of Camp Brotherhood.

Campers seek out a friendly cow. The Lamar McElroy family operate the farm and supervise Camp Brotherhood property. Ernie Engstrom, of the Cascade Catering Service, Kent, has personally supervised the kitchen since the Lodge was built.

A planning session for the Youth Services Project. Tacoma Area Urban Coalition, April 1974. From left, James S. Starr, W.A. "Tim" Burton, Jr., Al Morse and William G. Mitchell meet in the retreat house. Camp Brotherhood is used by a wide spectrum of the Pacific Northwest.

After campers retire, directors continue work in the multipurpose room of Fisher Lodge. Robert C. Brown, director of the Center for the Administration of Justice, University of California, and Jeanne Weaver, director of Youth Activities Department, HEW, participated in the Youth Services Project of the Tacoma Area Urban Coalition.

In 1963, Rabbi Levine, Father Treacy and Dr. Corson led a People-to-People tour from Seattle to Europe and the Middle East. For two months the group worked for greater understanding among peoples by getting to know people in other countries. From left: Harry Tall, Judge Charles Horowitz, Mrs. Margaret Smith, Mrs. Bernice Kaplan, Mrs. Diane Horowitz, Phil Kaplan, Mrs. Della Tall, the late Ed Pratt, Vice Admiral Hoge Smith, USN (ret.), Dr. Corson, Mrs. Reeva Levine, Rabbi Levine, Mr. and Mrs. Abe Poll, Benjamin Cole, Mrs. Kyran Hynes, travel agent Bob Wachtin, Perry Johannsen, Mrs. Hazel Cole, Mr. and Mrs. Larry Karrer, Mrs. Perry Johannsen, Dr. Kyran Hynes, Mrs. Dorothy Bullitt, Mr. and Mrs. Remick. On the stairs: Father Treacy, Mrs. Jeanette Tourtelotte, Mr. and Mrs. Merle Schenk, Mrs. Glenna Overton, Dean and Mrs. John Leffler, Mr. and Mrs. Fred Nielsen.

The CHALLENGE tour to Israel being seen off in New York on February 21, 1972 by El Al representative, Mrs. Harriet Steinberg (far left): Kneeling from left: Mrs. E.F. Penry, Mrs. Leo Bordeaux, Ray Dias, Jay Layton, Arthur Sternoff, Mrs. Robert Hunter, Mrs. John Riley; second row: Mrs. Eve Fields, Mrs. Ray Dias, Miss Evelyn Hall, Mrs. Patricia Bonnefield, Mrs. Dorothy Newman, Mrs. Elsa Mayer, Mrs. Elizabeth Gibson, Father Treacy, Rabbi Levine, Dr. Fine, Mrs. J. Ezra, the late Mrs. Tamara Sternoff, Mrs. Ida Goldfine, the late Mrs. Dorothy Martin, Dr. and Mrs. Norbert Trauba; back row: Mrs. Clara Kraft, Mrs. Genevieve Leverich, Mrs. Marie York, Mrs. George Paeth, Sister Patricia Jacobsen, Louis Bigge, Mrs. Hugh Harrison, Mrs. Dorothy Healey, Miss Carolyn Siegrist, Mrs. Jean Knutzen, Mrs. Louise Bigge. Absent: Mrs. Pat Guerin and television crew Tim Bullard, Willard Hatch, Lloyd Jones.

Judean hills are bleak and arid from centuries of pillaging the forests. Trees now grow in the Seattle Brotherhood Wood that inspired the CHALLENGE tour to Israel. The first trees were planted here on February 25, 1972 by Father Treacy, Rabbi Levine, Dr. Fine, Mrs. E.F. Penry and other tour members as Rabbi Moses Wyler, representing the Jewish National Fund, looks on.

(Photo by Willard Hatch)

When Father Treacy and Rabbi Levine were on the People-to-People tour in 1963, they were unable to visit the Wailing Wall together as the area where the Temple once stood was under Arab control. In 1972 they stood together at the Wall, significant because the lower rows of stones were a part of the Temple destroyed by the Romans in 70 A.D. Rabbi presided at a Bar Mitzvah at the Wall for an American boy who had gone there with his family as many do.

During the CHALLENGE tour, the panelists and crew made two CHALLENGE programs and a documentary in Israel and a CHALLENGE program in Rome. Willard Hatch begins "shooting" for the first one early one morning from the Mount of Olives. Father Treacy, Rabbi Levine and Dr. Fine look across the Kidron Valley to the city of Jerusalem.   (Photo by Tim Bullard)

One of the CHALLENGE programs was filmed outside Hebrew University with university students, both Jews and Arabs. One Jewish student was a recent arrival from Russia, one from the United States; another was born in Israel.
(Photo by Tim Bullard)

On the Mount of Beatitudes overlooking the Sea of Galilee, Father Treacy, Dr. Fine and Rabbi Levine read and comment on the Sermon on the Mount before CHALLENGE tour members Mrs. George Paeth, Dr. Norbert Trauba, Mrs. Jean Knutzen, Mrs. Ida Ezra and Mrs. Elsa Mayer.

Willard Hatch and Lloyd Jones against the Jerusalem skyline. The television crew was on the roof of Ecce Homo Convent to record work done at this cultural center affiliated with Hebrew University where Arabs and Jews learn one another's languages and study one another's cultures. The center is operated by the Catholic Sisters of Sion.   (Photo by Tim Bullard)

The night before leaving Jerusalem, Father Treacy celebrated Mass in the Lithostrotos, the excavated site of Jesus' condemnation, and many CHALLENGE tour members were present. Father used for the first time a carved olive wood chalice made by a Moslem carpenter and given him earlier in the day by Rabbi Levine.

(Photo by Tim Bullard)

At the peace greeting during the Mass, Father Treacy embraced Rabbi Levine and Dr. Fine and then all present, Catholics, Jews and Protestants, exchanged greetings with the panelists and with one another in a moving expression of unity.

(Photo by Tim Bullard)

Rabbi Levine, Mrs. Ida Goldfine, Mrs. Ida Ezra and Father Treacy visited Yad Vashem, the memorial to the six million Jews killed in the Holocaust during World War II. Here they stand on the grounds near the tall pylon built like a chimney. (Photo by Tim Bullard)

Producer Tim Bullard, cameraman Willard Hatch, audio-engineer Lloyd Jones and Dr. Robert Fine discuss filming possibilities. The crew, visiting Israel for the first time, had many on-the-spot discussions during the ten days of the tour.

The final CHALLENGE program of the tour was made in Rome and to open it, the panelists went to St. Peter's Basilica. (Photo by Tim Bullard)

and told us there were 50 monks in the monastery and some 240 students for the priesthood, ranging in age from 18 to 40. From the five seminaries operating in Russia, about a hundred priests were ordained each year to join the ranks of approximately 25,000 priests then serving the Russian people. Before we left, Brother Michael served us some exquisite kvass, a Russian liqueur, and we were each presented with an autographed book on Russian icons. In 1970 Archimandrite Pimen became Patriarch of the Russian Orthodox Church.

Ed Pratt of the Seattle Urban League, a Negro, who was later shot to death in his home, was a member of the People-to-People group. One day the two of us decided to take a stroll through the Kremlin. Kremlin means "fortress" and comprises government offices, a theatre, three churches preserved as museums, and souvenirs of the Communist Revolution. Russian tourists from the provinces visit the Kremlin as dutifully as the Catholic who goes to Rome visits the Vatican. A number of them stopped to photograph the Caucasian priest in clerical garb and the tall Negro walking together at a time when newspapers were giving much publicity to the plight of Negroes in America. Ed had a great sense of humor; he turned to me as we were being photographed and said, "Father, I think I will write an article when I get back to Seattle entitled *"Color and the Collar in the Kremlin"*.

On the morning of our departure from Moscow, Valentina was busy shepherding us through Customs and Immigration. When we were cleared, we assembled in a lounge to await the call to our plane for Vienna. Valentina joined me for coffee. During the week she had told me that her husband was on vacation at the Black Sea but because of the busy tourist season she was unable to accompany him. He was due home the previous evening. As we had coffee, I asked her if Igor got home. Tears came to her eyes and for a moment I saw desolation on her usual cheerful face. Soon she regained her composure and told me that he had arrived home the previous night but had contracted pneumonia on the long train journey. Since he had had it before she was afraid he was going to die. She had shown me pictures of their wedding a few years before and told me about their plans for the home and family they hoped to have and for which they were both saving.

With only minutes to visit, what can a Catholic priest say to a young atheist who is depressed by the thought of losing the man she loves? I did not have time to choose my words. I said, "Valentina, religion is not something negative in life. Part of your happiness with Igor was anticipation of the years ahead together. For a believer the anticipation adds still more joy for there is no end to the union. This is my faith. I wish I could share it with you now". She smiled gratefully, looked me in the eye and said, "I think I understand your faith". Then the flight to Vienna was called and we said goodbye.

A few years later a friend of mine, the late George Benson, Sr., was going to visit Moscow for the second time. He told me that his previous guide was most grateful for a subscription to National Geographic magazine. I suggested he check with the Intourist office on Gorky Street and if he was successful in finding Valentina, to offer her a subscription to National Geographic on behalf of the Seattle People-to-People tour. He did find her; she assured him she remembered the People-to-People tour from Seattle but when he told her about the gift we wished to present her, she replied, "Tell my Seattle friends I appreciate the offer but it is not necessary. I now believe the material gift passes away but the gift of the heart is forever."

Such experiences over a period of two months only heightened Rabbi's sorrow and mine at not being able to enter Jerusalem—

our common home—together. Our tour split in Athens and came together in Tel Aviv later. But heightened, too, was our resolve to heal the wounds that keep brothers apart.

8
Camp Brotherhood

One morning in the fall of 1966, Rabbi asked me to drive up to Mount Vernon with him to look over some property for a camp for Temple De Hirsch youth. I was already aware of his keen interest in camping; it was through spending his summers at a Jewish youth camp near Saratoga, California, that he got to know Reeva Miller, a distinguished artist from Santa Monica, who was art director at the camp. In 1959 he and Reeva were married. He had told me, too, details of his first camping experience at Seabeck on Hoods Canal in Washington where he was counselor for a week at a Christian religious camp. He left Seabeck inspired by what he had seen accomplished in just one intensive week of living, working, praying and playing together and was determined that Jewish youth should have the opportunity for such an experience. The Saratoga camp and others grew out of this determination.

Rabbi spoke with considerable excitement that day as we drove northward toward Mount Vernon. He had seen the property a day earlier with his friend, Alvin Schoenfeld, a land developer who was a member of the Temple. Called the Green Valley Farm, it was situated in Skagit County about 60 miles north of Seattle. After leaving the freeway, we drove for about eight miles on a good country road winding through the foothills of the Cascades to the farm just a quarter mile beyond lovely Lake McMurray. Just past the gate we came to a rise in the road from which we could look out over a lush valley of rolling meadowland surrounded by forested hills. Against one hill was a white farmhouse with a picket fence around it, a huge weatherbeaten barn and a number of sheds.

46

It was at this spot in the road the day before, Rabbi confided, that a much larger vision than a Temple camp came to him. He could see a great ecumenical religious, educational and cultural center for the Pacific Northwest coming into being in that glorious, secluded valley. It would be a spiritual oasis in the midst of the megalopolis which was growing so rapidly around us. It would be a retreat for the troubled spirit—for those seeking renewal to meet the challenges of a difficult world—for children, youth and families to learn to know each other as persons away from the turbulence and distractions of city life. It would be a haven for all who seek a deeper understanding of themselves and of their fellowmen. It would be a great center for conferences concerned with better human relations, for helping Americans to know each other in an atmosphere where they could live and plan and work together on equal terms for common purposes. It would become a place for study, for work, for recreation, for communication between people as they shared their knowledge and experience, their needs and hopes and dreams in the quiet inspiration of the soft meadows and deep forest glades—a place for thinking, dreaming, for companionship and solitude.

Would I be a part of this effort? People knew us from television; we represented brotherhood to them. If together we could found such a center, he was sure people would respond as they had in all our other efforts to bring diverse groups together.

Rabbi and Mr. Schoenfeld had talked to the owners, Mr. and Mrs. Leo Goldade, the day before and Rabbi had revealed his newly conceived dream. The Goldades already knew him from CHALLENGE and as they listened, Mr. Goldade's face clouded. He said he had already half promised to sell the property to a local purchaser who had placed $22,000 in escrow as a down payment. Seeing Rabbi so crestfallen, he hastened to add that the sale was not definite. The prospective buyer was waiting for his uncle from California who would have to supply the rest of the money and who was driving up to see the farm. Mr. Goldade promised that if this deal did not materialize, Rabbi could have first refusal of the property. Mr. Schoenfeld, also seeing what the farm meant to him, told him that if it was not sold, he could have any part or all of it and he and his land development friends would help him buy it.

We arrived at Green Valley Farm precisely at 9:30 to keep our appointment with the Goldades. They greeted us warmly and told us that the uncle of the prospective buyer had met with an accident in Oregon and that his nephew had gone to Portland to be with him. Mr. Goldade had told him about our interest in the farm and Rabbi's dream for its use. The man said that if we really wanted it for such a purpose, he would not stand in our way. The land could be ours if we could raise the money.

Rabbi is a dreamer but I know of no one who works harder to make his dreams come true. If his dream for Green Valley Farm was to be realized, we would need $85,000 to buy it with a down payment of $25,000 before he left for a conference in California three days later. But he firmly believed in brotherhood and this particular means to achieve it and he went from friend to friend sharing the vision and his enthusiasm for it. One gave $5,000, several $2,500 and $1,000. He borrowed $6,000 from the bank himself and when he got down to the last $2,500 he went to his sister, Ida Goldfine, knowing she would help him now as she had in so many ways and at so many times since their childhood in Vilna.

The property was secured and Mr. Goldade gave a contract at the rate of 6% interest, a generous concession in a money market that commanded much higher rates. The dream was now grounded in 320 wonderful acres surrounded by federal forest reserves and by tree farms of the Scott Paper Co. and the Puget Pulp Co., an oasis that commercialism was not likely to invade. Green Valley Farm thus became Camp Brotherhood.

The next step was to interest some of the leaders of the Seattle community in the project. A luncheon meeting hosted by Lowell Mickelwait, a Boeing vice-president, and William Woods, president of the Washington Natural Gas Co., was held on December 28, 1966 at the Washington Athletic Club. They sent out invitations to about 30 of Seattle's leaders and 24 came, representatives of a wide spectrum of the city's business and public life including managing editors of both daily newspapers. Rabbi and I were called upon to explain the purpose of Camp Brotherhood. During the question period we were challenged with the observation that it was a good idea but too ambitious and unrealistic. Rabbi hastened to reassure these leaders that what we had painted for them was a dream that might take 50 years to realize. We understood that beginnings must be slow. Mr. Woods and Mr. Mickelwait calmed the fears of the practical businessmen by assuring them that all they wanted was some kind of consensus on whether to even consider the idea in principle. The result of the meeting was a unanimous resolution that a non-profit corporation should be established to explore the feasibility of the project.

Three days later the story of Camp Brotherhood appeared on the front pages of both Seattle's daily newspapers. The *Seattle Post-Intelligencer* carried a banner headline that proclaimed "A Spiritual Oasis for the Skagit Valley". The purchase was news to the Temple Board; Rabbi had acted without consulting them because of previous refusals. But when the news broke, they gave him their support and it was the Temple De Hirsch that was first in building a retreat house for its young people at Camp Brotherhood.

Neither of us had thought of such mundane needs as water supply, sewage, building regulations, permits and a myriad of the other construction requirements we were to come to know well in the years ahead. Though we were still convinced of the need for a great living center for brotherhood, these requirements and the costs involved rose like nightmares to haunt us. It was toward the end of the first year after Camp Brotherhood Inc. was organized that the corporation took over the assets and liabilities of Unity Inc. which Rabbi had formed at the time of the purchase. Camp Brotherhood Inc. was now the sole owner of the 320 acres. But we still had no money or any line of credit at any bank with which to carry out an effective program. Nor did it seem likely that in the foreseeable future our financial position would improve.

Then one day Reeva remembered a young architect, Lee Copeland, who had worked with her at the Saratoga camp. He was now a professor in the School of Architecture at the University of Washington and a member of a firm with another professor, Robert Joyce. She invited them to visit Camp Brotherhood and met the architects and their families there for an outing one beautiful summer day. They became very excited with the beauty of the camp, our plans for it and the vision of its possibilities and agreed to make some sketches of how the property could be used, to show the Camp Brotherhood Inc. Board of Trustees.

This was the first great break-through. Another was meeting Tim Burton, executive director of the Washington region of the National Conference of Christians and Jews, who agreed to serve as the unsalaried executive director of the camp and who is responsible for much of its development.

A brotherhood camp was just the opportunity the NCCJ was looking for—a home—a center where the brotherhood ideal could come alive, where people could live brotherhood instead of merely talk about it on special formal occasions.

As interest in Camp Brotherhood grew, so did our dream of what it might become. Then in January 1968 the senior class of the University of Washington School of Architecture offered to design and build with their own hands a lodge for Camp Brotherhood. It was to be their class project for graduation, a new concept in architectural education, to give budding architects the opportunity to learn more than the theory of design and enable them to experience the practical problems of actual construction. They had heard of the camp and its goals from Professors Copeland and Joyce who were now making sketches for our Board of Trustees and they chose Camp Brotherhood for their project because the effort to build a better community appealed to their idealism and imagination.

They were invited to present their project at a special meeting of the Board of Trustees held in the Levine home. According to their estimates, a lodge to accommodate 60 persons would cost about $50,000 for materials only. They would donate their labor. The Board hesitated to make a firm commitment to the students and for a while it looked as if their gesture might die a-borning. It was then that Rabbi spoke up and told the Board that this was the moment of truth. If we were really interested in the development of Camp Brotherhood, we could not afford to reject this offer. But then perhaps the whole dream was a fantasy and we had better recognize it and accept it before we went any further. Faced with this challenge the Board unanimously voted to accept the students' offer and a committee headed by Winston D. Brown, president of the Howard Wright

Construction Co., was appointed to guide the 14 students in their construction work. They called their project "Environ '68".

For six months these young men worked without pay at Camp Brotherhood, often under the most difficult physical conditions, sleeping in the old farm house, eating what they could prepare themselves or what they brought from home. Occasionally the wives of those who were married would come to cook for them. Sometimes neighbors helped out. Four days a week they worked at the camp and two days at the university. June came, and graduation, and the building was unfinished. So seven of them under the leadership of Larry Craig, team captain, continued the work throughout the summer. Their contribution to Camp Brotherhood is commemorated by a bronze plaque bearing their names which now hangs on a wall of the multipurpose room in the building they created. On October 6, 1968, Governor Daniel Evans, honorary chairman of Camp Brotherhood, dedicated this three-story building which overlooks the valley and blends beautifully with the woods in which it is set.

Since that day in 1968, 40,000 people of all ages have used the lodge, among them members of the police force, drop-outs from high schools, college and high school students from all over Western Washington, retreat groups, boys' and girls' clubs, school staffs.

Playfields, trails, a pavilion, and picnic and campfire areas have been added, some constructed by young people who have stayed there and who bring their friends and family back to see their accomplishments.

The dream continues to expand. There will be a multipurpose building large enough for a concert center, a library with the kinds of books that help people get to know each other, other lodges, a swimming pool and tennis courts.

Someday the crude temporary "Camp Brotherhood" arch that now spans the entrance to the farm will be replaced by a sturdier one that will also include the words, "Children of a Common Father". The arch that gathers people together and sets them upon the same road recalls the reconciliation of man to God when God said to Noah after the destruction, "I set my bow in the cloud and it shall be a sign of the covenant between me and the earth". (Gen. 9:13)

9
Let Me Present My Friend

In the summer of 1971 the Personnel Board of the Seattle Archdiocese asked me if I would be willing to serve as a pastor outside Seattle, in Olympia. I hesitated to leave St. Patrick's parish, my friends in Seattle and the projects I had become involved in over 26 years. Rabbi and I met downtown for lunch one day to review the arguments for and against such a move. CHALLENGE was expanding to include other clergymen so it would not be necessary to come to Seattle every week or two to tape programs. St. Michael's in Olympia would mean a congregation twice the size of St. Patrick's, in a community small enough to be homogeneous but without the problems of a large metropolitan area. While there was personal loss to him in that our visits would have to be greatly curtailed, the Rabbi like a devoted father gave me his reassurance and his blessing. His words in the Seattle restaurant on a warm July day in 1971 echoed those of Ecclesiastes: "There is a season for everything . . . a time for planting . . a time for healing . . . a time for building . . . a time for tears." And for me, a time to move to Olympia. Thanks to Rabbi Levine who launched my television career, I did not go as a stranger to Olympia.

And now it is time I present to you Rabbi Raphael Levine who feels himself a stranger to no man.

Part Two

RABBI LEVINE

10

In a Russian Ghetto

As I look at the picture of myself with bowed head as my friend Father Treacy is celebrating Mass on an altar which I made for him at his request, I think back to my childhood in Vilna, originally the capital of Lithuania but at my birth belonging to Russia. When I recall the terrible fear I had of Christians, especially of the bearded, black-robed priests associated in my mind with the pogroms and persecutions of my people in their tragic experience in the Russian pale [2] settlements during the 17th, 18th and 19th centuries, and see myself—a rabbi—present at the central act of Christian worship led by a priest, I am amazed at the distance I have traveled from my childhood in the Russian ghetto in Vilna at the beginning of the 20th century to St. Patrick's Catholic Church in Seattle on March 17, 1965.

My first recollections of Christians were of Russian peasants who used to come to our house with their chickens and eggs and loads of bark for the tanneries which my father bought from them and sold in the local market place. Some of them were friendly and kind; but too often when they had indulged too freely in vodka they would become ugly and abusive, calling my father filthy names and heaping contempt upon him and all

---

(2) Areas in which Jews were permitted to live without permission were called the pale. Outside the pale only by special permission were carefully selected Jews permitted to dwell and carry on their business or profession.

Jews and Judaism. When at seven I was old enough to go to a Russian school I became a special target for the Christian boys to taunt and abuse with their favorite epithet, "Zhid", almost the equivalent of "Sheeny" but worse. It was the Christmas and Easter holidays that were especially trying for Jews in the Russian pale. These were times when Russian peasants, informed by their priests of the Jew's role in the crucifixion of Jesus as sermonically embellished from the New Testament account, became especially ugly in their anger at the Jewish "Christ killers" and made the Jews in their neighborhoods the victims of their holy zeal for revenge. It was at these times I remember that we would bolt our doors and shutter our windows and stay indoors for fear of the drunken peasants who often terrorized the ghetto. Some of the most tragic pogroms were engineered during these holy days. So my childhood experience with Christianity and Christians was full of fears; and the very word "Christ" became a synonym for tragedy in the Jew's vocabulary, and for me as a child a word which to utter was a grievous sin.

I was born in 1901 in Vilna, the youngest of 12 children of whom four had died before I was born. When I came into the world, four sisters and three brothers were there to greet me. Since no birth records were kept we never really knew the exact date. It was only when I was approaching my 13th birthday and had to go through the ceremony of being inducted into religious manhood as a Bar Mitzvah (Son of the Commandments) according to our Jewish tradition that it became important to fix an exact date. This was necessary to determine what Torah portion I had to read. By diverse family events and relationships at the time of my birth, they calculated that my Bar Mitzvah must occur around the middle of August because my *Maftir*, which is the portion the Bar Mitzvah boy reads from the Torah, happened to coincide with the Sabbath nearest August 15, 1914. So I took August 15 as my official birthday and that is what it is to this day.

The home in which we lived in Vilna was a wooden, thatched duplex with a balustrade dividing the porch and separating the two dwellings. Our part had two rooms. One was a multipurpose room containing a large brick oven which served as a dining, kitchen, family room and my father's business office; the other was divided by a curtain into two bedrooms, one of them for my maternal grandmother who lived with us. My two nephews and I slept on top of the warm brick oven which extended from the front room to the back wall of the house. The house was lighted by kerosene lamps and the floor was of dirt, covered with sawdust.

I remember how before dawn the peasants would start coming with their products. The walls of our house were whitewashed and there was one wall which was used as a kind of ledger where my father would mark down with charcoal strokes the amounts of merchandise each peasant brought. In this primitive way accounts were kept since most of the peasants were illiterate and unable to understand written numbers.

Ever since I can remember, my grandmother lived with us and took care of me while my parents worked. I knew my grandfather only from a photograph, which showed a patriarch with a long, forked beard. He was known as "Lebel the Innkeeper" in his village of Mushnik, not far from Vilna, and held an office equivalent to mayor. He died at the age of 104 and my grandmother, already in her 80's, came to live with my mother, the eldest of her 15 children.

At a very early age, probably at about four as was the custom among the Jews of the ghetto, I was inducted into my Hebrew education by being taught the Hebrew alphabet. We had a teacher who came to our home to instruct me and my youngest sister, Ida, who was seven years older than I. It was the tradition that when a boy began his first lesson the book was opened and a little honey was placed on the first page to symbolize the sweetness of study. When I was six I went to the Heder, or Hebrew school, where I spent most of the day from eight in the morning to mid-afternoon. I still recall what my first teacher looked like. He was a thin, hunched man, with a scraggly beard and dark, brooding eyes. He wore a long coat, the sleeves of which were greasy with long use as a handkerchief. He was very strict with us children and if we did not know our lessons he would stab us in the shoulder with his two forefingers hard enough to cause considerable pain.

Our home was in the ghetto on the outskirts of the city. Across the road from the house was a large open area with wooded hills. At regular intervals the military garrison at Vilna came here for maneuvers. These were exciting days seeing the military wagons rumbling past our house and the soldiers playing at war in the open fields, shouting as they charged up and down the hills.

The most pleasant memories of my childhood were of the Sabbath and the religious holidays. On Friday my father would come home from work about noon, and my mother, who usually worked right along with him, stayed home all day to prepare for the Sabbath. That was the time when Mother baked the twisted loaves of white bread known as *challah*. White bread was a luxury reserved for the Sabbath and festivals. There had to be at least two loaves to symbolize the double portion of manna which the ancient Hebrews collected on the eve of the Sabbath so that they would not have to collect their daily portion on the Sabbath and so violate the commandment against working on the Sabbath day. Also food had to be prepared not only for the Sabbath eve dinner on Friday but for the entire next day when cooking was prohibited.

The observance of the Sabbath was the high point of every week. My parents did not have to work. There was special food reserved for this wonderful day. Each Friday, my mother would have a peasant woman come to the house to clean and make it spotless. Instead of the usual sawdust on the floor, fine white sand was spread about and the white walls were scrubbed clean, especially the wall that was used for accounting purposes. As Mother began her baking and cooking a heavenly aroma pervaded the whole house. The Sabbath was an occasion when she prepared special dishes including a kind of ravioli called *kreplach* which was filled with ground meat and boiled in chicken soup.

On Sabbath eve the table was set with our best linen, china and silver. There were always two brass candlesticks which were given to my mother as a wedding present by her parents. The two candles had to be lit on the eve of the Sabbath as a symbol of the light and joy which the Sabbath brought into Jewish life. At each place at the table was also a silver beaker for wine used for the *kiddush* prayer sanctifying the Sabbath.

While Mother was busy preparing the house and the food to honor the Queen Sabbath, as it was called in our Jewish tradition, my father and I would go to the Finnish sauna and take our weekly bath. We had no indoor plumbing at home. We would come home scrubbed clean and put on our best Sabbath clothes, and then my father and I would go to the synagogue for the Sabbath service, which centered on the beauty of the Sabbath and thanksgiving to God for all his bounty to us during the week. At the synagogue we would usually pick up a stranger as a guest to share our Sabbath joy. Strangers, away from home, and professional beggars would come to the synagogue for the Sabbath services knowing that they would receive hospitality from the regular worshipers. Every Jew considered it a privilege to have one or more guests to share his Sabbath joy.

Arriving home, the first thing that father would do was to greet my mother with the traditional poem idealizing Jewish womanhood as found in the 31st chapter of the Book of Proverbs: "A woman of worth, who can find. Her price is far above rubies. The heart of her husband does safely trust in her and she doeth him good and not evil." After greeting Mother, Father would bless each of us children. Then we would sit down to the Sabbath meal that began with the *kiddush* prayer:

> Let us praise God with this symbol of joy, and thank Him for the blessings of the past week, for life and strength, for home and love and friendship, for the discipline of our trials and temptations, for the happiness that has come to us out of our labors. Thou hast ennobled us, O God, by the blessings of work, and in love hast sanctified us by Sabbath rest and worship as ordained in the Torah: Six days shalt thou labor and do all thy work, but the seventh day is the Sabbath to be hallowed unto the Lord, thy God.

> Praised be Thou, O Lord our God, King of the Universe, who hast created the fruit of the vine.

Then breaking a piece of the *challah*, Father prayed: "Blessed art Thou, O Lord our God, who brings forth bread from the earth". He cut one loaf into pieces and distributed a piece to each person at the table. With this ritual completed the dinner was served—first the soup, then the entree, usually chicken, then a thick stew of potatoes, carrots and prunes called *tzimmes* and finally, sponge cake and tea. Before the grace after meals came the *zmiros*, the singing of selected psalms and traditional Sabbath songs. In the final grace, we thanked God that we had been blessed with the privilege of observing the Sabbath and had been recipients of God's bounty, grateful that we were not dependent on men but always on God for life and everything that enabled us to enjoy it.

By the time the meal was over, and often before it was finished, I was ready for bed, sometimes falling asleep while eating. But the older children and adults remained at the table carrying on conversation which usually turned on a discussion of Torah, instruction from the Bible, or events of the week.

On Saturday morning we were able to stay in bed a little longer. My mother, however, was already up preparing breakfast for my father and me when we got up so that we would not be delayed in going to the synagogue for the morning worship. The synagogue was a wooden structure about a mile from our home. We walked, of course, since riding was forbidden on the Sabbath, because the animals, too, had to have their day of rest. My father took his accustomed place near the Ark, a position given to the more respected members of the community. The service from eight o'clock in the morning till noon was very long for young children and so during the long reading of the weekly Torah portion, we children went outside to play.

Returning home we were greeted by the fragrant aroma of *cholent*, a one-dish meal of meat and vegetables kept warm overnight in the banked oven. After a leisurely midday meal, my father would ask me what I had learned in Hebrew school during the week and examine me to see how much I really had learned. Much of the afternoon I spent in play with my friends. Father would read the Torah portion again and Mother, a translation known as *Tzenah Urenah* which means *Go and See* —a book prepared for women containing wisdom literature and legends important in Jewish history. Usually my parents would take a nap, a luxury impossible during the busy week. Late in the afternoon, Father and I returned to the synagogue where we sometimes heard a *maggid*, a traveling preacher who went from town to town giving ethical and inspirational sermons. Usually there were men studying Torah or Talmud, the rabbinic commentary on the Bible, led by some of the more learned men of the community if no rabbi was available. By this time the sun was setting and it was time for *Mincha*, the afternoon service, always rather hurried and followed immediately by the evening service, *Maariv*. This ended the Sabbath observance in the synagogue but at home there was still the *Havdalah*.

The *Havdalah* service was mingled with gratitude and sadness. We were very reluctant to see the Sabbath end, with the toilsome week before us for the next six days. Father would take us outside, weather permitting, to watch for the first sign of moonrise, the signal for the beginning of the *Havdalah* service. The ritual included lighting a twisted candle and dipping the candle flame in a saucer of wine. Over each act Father would recite a blessing, thanking God for the creation of light and for the fruit of the vine, and then he would sniff a spice box, symbolizing the fragrance and beauty of the Sabbath, thanking God for creating all kinds of spices. With this ritual completed the Sabbath came to an end and we sat down to the evening meal, which was not so festive as any of the previous meals. The week of toil and trouble lay ahead.

11
Religious Feasts and Fasts

Judaism is rich in festivals and holydays, each with its own special significance and each bringing to my childhood experience new wonders to look forward to through the year. The most glamorous of these was the Passover commemorating the deliverance from slavery in Egypt by Moses. It came in the springtime of the year. Passover was exciting with the whole pattern of life changed. It was a time for cleaning the house of every vestige of leavened bread, a time for the most thorough spring cleaning, for eating unleavened bread, *matzo*, and the special delicacies reserved only for Passover. A complete set of china was brought out of storage where it had been packed in straw since last Passover to be used only for this festival. In the ghetto where we lived there were several bakeries that specialized in the baking of *matzo*. It was exciting to go with my parents to the bakery and watch them have our *matzo* baked and then cart it home in huge white sacks. One part of the house was prepared to receive the *matzo*. There, in preparation for Passover, some of it would be pounded into flour and what particles were left were used in chicken soup like croutons. It was always a thrill for me when Mother allowed me to help pound *matzo* into flour with a wooden pestle.

Highlight of the Passover festival was the Seder feast and the night was made for me. For weeks I had prepared to inaugurate the Passover celebration by chanting the traditional four questions, the special privilege of the youngest male child: "Why is this night different from all other nights? On all other nights we may eat either leavened or unleavened bread; why on this night do we eat only unleavened bread? On all other nights we eat all kinds of herbs; why on this night do we eat only bitter herbs?

On all other nights we do not dip herbs in any condiment; why on this night do we dip them in salt water and *haroses?* On all other nights we eat without any special festivities; why on this night do we hold this Seder service?" Then my father would read through the whole story of how our forefathers suffered as slaves in Egypt and how Moses delivered them by performing wonderful miracles.

One responsibility I always looked forward to was carrying the *haroses,* a paste made of apples, nuts and honey to every family in our neighborhood. My father had the reputation for being the best *haroses* maker in our area and I got to deliver the delicacy for which I was rewarded with a small coin from each recipient. The mud-like appearance of the paste symbolized the mortar which the Hebrew slaves used to make bricks in their forced labor of constructing the cities and monuments for their Egyptian masters.

In the annual cycle of our religious calendar, the festival following seven weeks after Passover was Shabuoth, the Feast of Weeks, a two-day holiday commemorating the revelation of God to Moses on Mount Sinai, a revelation embodied in the Ten Commandments described in the Book of Exodus. Originally, Shabuoth (or Pentecost as it is sometimes called because it occurs 50 days after Passover) was a farmers' festival when the first ripe fruit was gathered and brought as a gift to the Temple in Jerusalem as part of an annual spring pilgrimage to the Holy City. Later it was identified with the revelation on Sinai and commemorates the covenant which God made with our forefathers 3500 years ago. Today it is celebrated in Reform congregations, and increasingly in some Conservative and Orthodox congregations, as a time for the confirmation of boys and girls who at 15 or older wish to publicly accept the faith of their fathers into

which they were born and to make their own personal commitment to it.

Another very joyous holiday was Hanukah, the festival of
lights. It was celebrated for eight days and commemorated the
seemingly miraculous victory in 168 B.C. of the Maccabeans
over their Greek overlords who tried to force the Jews to give up
their Judaism and to adopt the Greek gods and forms of worship. During the eight days of the festival, candles were lit in
the *menorah*, one on the first night, two on the second and one
additional candle each night until all eight were glowing.

Legend tells us that after the Maccabees had driven the
Greeks out of Jerusalem, they cleansed the Temple of all the
pollution the Greeks had caused during their occupation and
held a service of thanksgiving and rededication of the Temple to
the service of God. Holy oil was required for the service but
none was available. A little boy playing in the restored Temple
found a tiny jar of oil that still bore the unbroken seal of the
High Priest who officiated before the Greeks took over. The jar
contained only enough oil for one day but by a miracle it lasted
for eight days until new oil could be produced. The eight
candles of the *menorah* recall this miracle.

Hanukah was a happy time. We children could look forward
to gifts, usually money all our own to spend any way we liked.
There were also Hanukah games. My favorite was spinning the
dreidel, a small square top made of lead with Hebrew letters on
each of the four sides. Each letter represented a word in the
sentence "God wrought a great miracle here". If after spinning,
the top fell on certain letters, it meant that the spinner had to
put one of his Hanukah kopeks (pennies) in the pot; if it fell on
others, he was entitled to take a kopek out.

Purim, which occurs about a month before Passover, is
another exciting festival for children. It commemorates the de-

liverance of the Jews of Persia in the reign of Artaxerxes from the evil designs of Haman, prime minister of Persia. The Book of Esther tells how Haman decided that the Jews ought to be eliminated from the Persian empire because their religion was different from the rest of the people and they were an unassimiable group within the body politic. So with the approval of the king he decreed their destruction. However, his nefarious plans were frustrated by Esther, who in a beauty contest was chosen queen of Persia, without the king's knowing that the queen he had chosen was a Jewess. She revealed her identity during this critical period and the king's love for her was so great that he had Haman hanged on the gallows prepared for Esther's uncle, Mordecai, the leader of the Jewish community. Mordecai's and the Jews' divine deliverance was joyously celebrated in the synagogue by reading the story of Esther and by an exchange of gifts. As the story of Esther was read, every time the name of Haman was mentioned there was a stamping of feet and other noise to show contempt for this arch anti-Semite who met his just deserts in that time long ago, and every time Mordecai's name was mentioned there was applause. For us children it was a great opportunity to let go without fear of punishment.

The High Holydays were of special significance. Traditionally the New Year and the Day of Atonement, known as the Days of Awe, were regarded as the time when every person's life was examined and judged by a heavenly court as to whether the individual was to be rewarded or punished for his conduct during the year. The New Year was the day of reckoning; the Day of Atonement, the time when the verdict was rendered. Between the New Year and Day of Atonement were ten days for repentance, for making amends to friends and neighbors for wrongs done to them and asking their forgiveness. Tradition has it that the penitential season will atone only for sins against

God, ritual infractions or unfulfilled vows made to God in times of stress. Wrongs committed against one's fellowmen were not forgiven on the Day of Atonement unless the wrongdoer had made every possible effort to right the wrong he had committed by making restitution and seeking the wronged person's forgiveness. I remember my father going out in preparation for the Day of Atonement to every neighbor to beg forgiveness for every wrong he had done knowingly or through oversight or accident.

The Holydays were awe-inspiring for both adults and children; but for me they were a time for new winter clothes in preparation for the approaching Russian winter, in Vilna always very severe. Then there were the special goodies Mother would prepare for the New Year which always included apples and honey to symbolize the hope for a sweet and happy year ahead. Sometimes we even got an orange, a rare treat in the ghetto.

Five days after the Day of Atonement came the Feast of Tabernacles. This was the autumn harvest festival among the ancient Hebrews, when they gathered their grapes, wheat and autumn fruits and vegetables and gave thanks to God that they would have enough food until the next harvest. During the season the Hebrew farmers used to build shelters to protect themselves from the burning midday sun. These were called *succoth* and they became a symbol of the festival and gave it its name Hag Hasuccoth, the Festival of Booths (Tabernacles). To symbolize and commemorate these shelters my father, and every pious Jew in the community, built a wooden hut in his backyard with four walls, a door and a roof of evergreen branches. The idea of the hut was interpreted in later tradition to symbolize the frailty of man and life and his dependence on God.

If the weather was not too inclement we would eat our meals in the *succah* during the eight days of festival. If the weather

was bad, my father would take us there for the blessing sanctifying the occasion and then we would go into the house for our
meal. It was always exciting to help my father at the end of the
Day of Atonement when he came from the synagogue, before he
tasted anything after his 24-hour fast, drive a stake into the
ground where the *succah* would be erected.

The last day of Succoth was Simchat Torah, rejoicing for the
Torah. During Simchat Torah all boys under 13, at the end of
the reading of the Torah, were gathered under a large *tallit*
(prayer shawl) and while thus covered by it the blessing over the
reading of the Torah was recited on their behalf by the cantor.
Boys who had attained the age of 13 and become Bar Mitzvah
were already regarded as adults for religious purposes and could
wear their own *tallit* and recite the blessing themselves.

Simchat Torah was the only time of the year that a Jew was
allowed to drink strong liquor to the point where he could not
distinguish between the need to bless Mordecai and curse
Haman, the traditional hero and villain of the Purim story. It
was also a time in our ghetto community when the Torahs were
carried around the synagogue in a festive procession and we
children were given paper flags to carry around as we marched
with the elders. Another highlight of the Simchat Torah celebration was the progressive dinner after the morning service
when we danced through the streets of the ghetto and went
from house to house eating a different course in each house and
ending the festival in a kind of carnival spirit.

There were many difficulties to be endured in the Russian
ghetto, but there was also much happiness and fulfillment in the
festive observances of our religious year.

12
America—The Promised Land

When I was five we had a frightening visit from the police. It was during the Russian Revolution of 1905. My brother, Louis, then 23 and a harness-maker by trade, belonged to an organization called the "Bund", a kind of labor union agitating for more rights for the working man. During the Revolution and after, every suspected Bund member was rounded up as a subversive. Louis was arrested in a restaurant where he and some of his friends had gathered, and taken to jail. The police searched the house for weapons and seditious literature. I was very small for my age and one policeman especially was like a towering giant and terrified me. They came during Purim when it is traditional to make a lot of noise and I was playing with a toy cap pistol. The giant grabbed hold of me and said in a gruff voice, "I'm dragging you off to prison. I see you have a revolver and you are a very dangerous person". Then he laughed.

The shock of my brother being in jail with the possibility of being tried as a revolutionary and sent to Siberia was traumatic for the family. For nine months he was in jail awaiting trial. We visited him as often as we could. One day Ida, at that time about twelve, made her way into the city alone to plead with the governor of the province for Louis' release. I really do not know whether it was her plea to the governor or other circumstances that persuaded him to release Louis. But he was released and he and Ida with two of our nephews whose parents were already in America, left Vilna to join them and a married brother, Max.

I was left alone with my father and mother, and the house seemed awfully big and terribly empty. My parents had already decided that they would follow as soon as they were able to arrange their affairs. About two years later they sold everything we had and we set out to join our family going first to Libau, the large Latvian seaport on the Baltic. There we took a ship for England. I was then eight years old.

We landed in Liverpool, England, during the Succoth festival and my father took me to the Orthodox synagogue in Liverpool to worship. Strange how life deals with us. Twenty-four years later I became rabbi of this same synagogue which my first congregation, the Liberal Jewish congregation of Liverpool, had purchased and transformed into a Reform synagogue.

After waiting about a week in Liverpool, we went to South-hampton to board the ship that was to take us to America, and found our place in steerage with other immigrants. Since my family was strictly Orthodox and observed all the dietary regulations we ate no food on the ship that was not *kosher*. My mother had prepared for the voyage large hampers of food to last the nine days. The only things I remember eating on the ship not brought by my mother were hard-boiled eggs, bread, jam and tea.

We arrived in Quebec and were quarantined, like prisoners, in a wire enclosed stockade. I remember some beautifully dressed ladies from the Jewish community coming to visit us and bringing us fruit and other goodies. After quarantine and customs we boarded a train for Duluth, Minnesota. There, we were greeted by our now American family and it was an intensely emotional experience, a mingling of joy, tears and laughter.

My two nephews, one my age and one three years older, were already quite Americanized since they had been in the country two years and spoke English like Americans. I regarded them with awe. They took me in hand and began my Americanization process. First they gave me an American name. My name in

Hebrew is Raphael, but my nephews thought that was no name for an American. The best American names, they told me, were Tom, Dick and Harry. They decided that Harry would be a good one for me. So Harry I became—and remained until I graduated from high school. It was when we were asked to designate how we wanted our names inscribed on our diplomas that I felt sufficiently Americanized to take my real name, though I shortened it to Ralph, using Harry as a middle name. The metamorphosis of my name from Harry to Ralph to Raphael came when I was graduated from the University of Minnesota Law School. I was then already contemplating the possibility of becoming a rabbi. I felt that the name Raphael, which means "God the Healer", was more appropriate for one who had aspirations to be a Jewish religious leader. I still retain the "H" as my middle initial.

Duluth was a city of about 100,000 in 1909. My father, mother and I were settled in a house which Louis and Ida had rented for the family in Chester Park where there were a number of Jewish families. Our wooden house was situated on one of the hills on Sixth Street about three blocks from a lovely wooded area with a creek running through it. To us children this was a wonderland of adventure, eminently suited for our war games since it had a ravine and woods and one could ambush the enemy and hide from him easily.

In Vilna my father had been of some importance, being a petty broker and by ghetto standards, fairly successful. Here in Duluth, handicapped by not knowing the language, already in his 50's and having no particular skill, he had no alternative but to become a junk collector as many immigrants before him had. My mother, of course, could not work as she was even more handicapped by language than he and she had a full-time job taking care of our home.

Peddling merchandise required some capital which we did not have and so each day my father took a sack and went about the neighborhood collecting whatever junk he might get for nothing or for a small sum, toiling up steep Duluth hills toward nightfall with a heavy sack full of junk. After months of this back-breaking work, Louis and Ida bought him a child's coaster wagon, the biggest they could get. My father became a familiar figure in our neighborhood as he dragged his wagon through the streets. In this way he was able to eke out a living which my brother and sister supplemented with their wages, Louis as harness-maker and Ida in a sweater factory. One of the memories that grieves me most is being so ashamed at seeing my father with his wagon that I would take another way home.

I was enrolled in a grammar school about a half mile from our home and supervised by Miss Calverly, a plump, motherly principal whom I shall never forget for her interest in my welfare. She took the little immigrant boy to her heart and helped me during the most difficult first years of American schooling, trying to learn the language and mastering the curriculum of the primary grades. I was much older than my classmates and through her personal interest I was able to close some of the age gap between myself and them by skipping grades. Even though I did eight grades in five years, I was still older than any of my classmates on graduation.

While attending grammar school I helped to supplement the family income by selling newspapers, shining shoes and singing in the synagogue choir. I am very proud that the first suit of clothes I bought in America I paid for with my own earnings as a choir boy. I was paid $2 for my services. The suit I bought, a tweed knickerbocker with norfolk jacket, cost $1.98. I also helped my mother take care of two cows we now owned. My job was to help clean the stable, deliver the fresh milk to our customers and do some chores around the house. My father was doing quite well as a junk dealer and began to take his proper place in the synagogue which we attended.

All through grammar school, Miss Calverly was my staunch friend and confidant. Through her I learned to love America and Americans and the fear of Christians which I brought with me from the Russian ghetto gradually disappeared. I even got to the point of becoming Miss Calverly's personal messenger delivering her Christmas cards and presents to her friends, without feeling that I was betraying my own Jewish faith. During my grammar school years I made a number of Christian friends who also helped me overcome my fears. I began to learn that there were all kinds of Christians, that while there were still boys who taunted me as "Sheeny" there were others who were ready to defend me even to the point of fighting with others. I was in America now and this awareness was reassuring and heart-warming.

13
Teacher—Lawyer—Rabbi

I was very small for my age and continually haunted by the fear that I would be a dwarf. But I had a strong voice so that even as a child of ten, I was able to recite at our school assembly and make myself heard by large audiences. When at 13 I became Bar Mitzvah and entered into religious manhood, my rabbi wrote a long speech for me, which must have been his philosophy of life, and I delivered it from memory during the synagogue service. You can imagine the astonishment of the congregation on hearing profound religious ideas proclaimed in a booming voice by a little fellow who could hardly reach the top of the podium. This gift for oratory channeled my interest in high school and in college toward becoming a lawyer. My concept of the law as a profession was to stand before a jury and make eloquent pleas for my client. I thought all that was necessary was to have average intelligence, a good voice and, in the vernacular, "the gift of gab". I had all three.

After graduating from high school and completing a two-year teacher training course in Superior, Wisconsin, I went to the University of Minnesota in 1922 to prepare to enter law school. While there I became interested in a Jewish student organization called the Menorah Society. This was a cultural organization which flourished on many campuses in the United States but has since been supplanted by the Hillel Foundation. It was designed to enhance the social and cultural life of Jewish students. In my senior year I became its president and during my term we had a number of debates and symposia discussing Jewish life and Jewish survival. We debated with Menorah societies of other universities and had groups speaking at B'nai B'rith meetings and to other Jewish organizations in Minnesota.

In order to prepare for these debates and symposia, I found it necessary to learn more about Judaism and especially Jewish history, a subject which had been neglected in my Jewish education.

The only Jewish education I had in the Hebrew School was to learn how to read the Hebrew prayer book, to translate the Bible from Hebrew into English, and a little of the rabbinic commentaries on the Bible. The Hebrew school I attended in Duluth five afternoons a week after school emphasized the capacity for speed in reading Hebrew and memorizing prayers. All the canons of education I have learned since were violated. Of the 4000-year history of our people, I knew almost nothing. The little biblical history we got in our Hebrew school was garbled and, to me, had little meaning. So when I had to learn about Jews and Judaism to prepare for the discussions on what it means to be a Jew and the problems of Jewish existence and survival in a non-Jewish world, I found it necessary to begin reading the history of the Jews. My sister, Ida, with whom I lived in Minneapolis during my university years, seeing my interest and need, gave me the classic *History of the Jews* by Heinrich Greaetz, translated into English from German and published by the Jewish Publications Society in a popular edition of five volumes.

I was fascinated by Professor Greaetz's vivid style and marvelous capacity for narrative, so that I read the five volumes, one after the other as one reads an absorbing novel. It gave me an insight into Judaism and an understanding of my people I had never had before and this experience changed the course of my life. I continued to study law but I was already beginning to think in terms of devoting my life to Judaism and the Jewish people.

What strengthened this interest leading to my decision to become a rabbi was a conversation I had with the dean of our law school just before graduation. I had enjoyed the study of law and also liked teaching and so I thought I might make teaching law my career. I consulted the dean about the possibility of doing postgraduate work with the aim of becoming a university professor. He was very kind and quite frankly told me that what concerned him was that I was a Jew and while there were some outstanding Jewish law professors, a Jew had to be exceptionally brilliant to attain a professorship at a recognized university law school. This was in 1926.

Fortunately I was enough aware of my limitations to know that while I may have been above average as a student, I was not exceptional. I have never ceased being grateful to Dean Fraser for his honest evaluation of my situation. I finished law school, passed the Bar examinations the first time I took them and returned to Duluth to practice law.

As was the custom among young legal graduates, I tried to get a position with a good law firm and found the going difficult. So I decided to go into private practice with a boyhood friend, Henry Paul (born Polinsky), who had graduated the same year as I had from the University of Michigan Law School.

Henry Paul was a tall, gaunt, Lincolnesque figure of a man with an excellent mind and a fine sense of humor. He was a lovable person—kind, generous to a fault, with a highly sensitized social conscience. We had been close boyhood friends and now that we were both young lawyers on our own, we decided to enter into a partnership to save expenses in operating a law office. Business came very slowly and our practice was largely a matter of collecting debts for our clients, garnisheeing some poor debtor's wages, drawing up an occasional contract or helping in the probate of some small estate of a friend or member of our families. We hardly made enough to pay the modest rent on our office space. Henry had one fault, grievous to me, which was the only flaw in our relationship. He had no sense of time and rarely kept appointments without making the person he was to meet wait what seemed an unconscionable time. I was—and still am—a compulsive time keeper. This became a source of irritation between us, so that while we kept the same office we dissolved our partnership and each carried on his own practice. Our friendship, however, remained close and fast until I left Duluth to study for the rabbinate.

Even while practicing law, my real interests were in working within the Jewish community. I organized study groups among my friends and in the Orthodox synagogue to which my father belonged. These absorbed my attention almost to the neglect of the little law practice that came to me. After about nine months of this conflict of interest between my law work and my teaching, I became convinced that even if I were successful in the law, my heart was not in it. My real interest was in teaching. Law might give me a better living than teaching but what I wanted above everything at that time was personal self-fulfillment which I then felt I could never attain in the law. In Judaism, working with my people for the things which Judaism had taught me were the important values of life for me at least, made me realize that I would be able to find the kind of fulfillment and self-expression I sought only by becoming a rabbi. I cannot say that I received what some feel was a call to the rabbinate, nor as I look back upon my decision to give up the law and to go to a rabbinical seminary was I motivated by any great religious fervor. My faith in God was conventional and rather nebulous; but this I knew with a growing conviction, that in teaching Judaism and in helping my people to understand their heritage I would find my mission in life and the road to self-fulfillment.

As I look back on my decision from the vantage point of 40 years as a rabbi, I can say that if I had my life to live over, knowing everything I now know of the rabbinate with all its difficulties and heartaches, frustrations and disappointments, I would still want to be a rabbi. I am grateful for the choice I made in 1927.

14
Hebrew Union College

I decided to go to Hebrew Union College in Cincinnati, the seminary for training Reform rabbis. Although I was reared in the Orthodox tradition, Orthodox Judaism with its rigid dietary discipline and its ultraconservative attitudes toward change no longer appealed to my searching mind. Reform Judaism and the Reform rabbinate offered for me the largest measure of religious freedom in thought and action.

I spent five years at Hebrew Union College. I was 26 when I entered, eight years older than the average freshman who came to the college from high school. The course of study was four years in the preparatory department and four in the graduate, but because of my previous education I spent only one year in the preparatory department. There were about 116 students at the College when I began my studies in 1927, divided fairly equally between the two departments. I was older on entering than most of the seniors that year.

Because I was so much older than my classmates, I was very much alone the first two years. In my third year I met a young woman who had come to Cincinnati from Portland, Oregon, to live with her older sister, Irma Cohon the wife of the professor of theology at the College. She was a graduate of the School of Social Work at the University of Washington. We met through Professor Samuel Cohon who told me that his sister-in-law, Madeline Reinhart, was looking for someone to teach her Yiddish that she might better communicate with many of the clients of the local Jewish social agency where she worked.

I don't know whether I was a successful teacher, but within a few months, Madeline and I became engaged and in 1929 we were married in a simple ceremony in the study of a famous

79

Chicago rabbi, Tobias Schanfarber. After a honeymoon of one weekend mostly atop a sight-seeing bus in Chicago, we returned to Cincinnati. I left the dormitory where I had lived my first two years at the seminary and we set up housekeeping in a small apartment. Madeline continued her work in the social agency and I got a position as assistant editor of a new Anglo-Jewish weekly appropriately named *Every Friday* since it came out every week on the eve of the Sabbath. With the money I earned at *Every Friday* and what Madeline earned as a social worker, we managed quite well. About a year and a half after our marriage, our daughter Lori Jean was born. Madeline had to give up her work but by then I was a full-fledged editor of *Every Friday* earning about $2000 a year on a part-time basis. This salary combined with money I earned from Sunday school teaching at a local Temple and a students' bi-weekly congregation at Richmond, Indiana came to about $3000.

I was kept running during the last two years at the College what with editing the paper, taking a full course at the College, teaching Sunday school and holding a student bi-weekly position at Richmond. To keep up this split second schedule, especially between my editorial work and classes, I bought our first car, an ancient Chevrolet for which I paid $150. Often I ate my lunch in the car driving from school to my office and from the office to classes—sometimes a sandwich I brought from home, most often wolfing a hamburger from one of the popular stand-up snack bars which proliferated in Cincinnati at that time.

This kind of hectic daily routine was not conducive to good health, equanimity or good scholarship. Many a time I fell asleep in class, not always from exhaustion. Sometimes it was the soothing drone of some professor's monotonous monologue. However, I managed to survive and even to win a scholarship prize in my senior year. This was due more perhaps to the generosity of one of my professors than to my scholastic achievement. He was Dr. Abraham Cronbach, of blessed memory, to whom I owe more than I shall ever be able to repay, not merely for his kindness but for what I learned from him.

Abraham Cronbach was an unusual man. He was a rabbi, a graduate of the College in which he became professor of social studies. To many of the students he was known as the "automatic saint", because he was soft-spoken, ascetic and meticulous in word and action. He was a liberal in thought, even radical, and given to iconoclastic ideas about organized religion. His interpretation of Judaism was in the tradition of the great Hebrew prophets, emphasizing the ethical and moral values in religion above everything. He was probably unique among Jewish religious leaders of his time in that he was an absolute pacifist, and before World War II became the founder of the Jewish Peace Fellowship, a pacifist group within Judaism.

Dr. Cronbach was precise in his speech and most careful in his use of words. From him I learned the importance of the careful use of words to convey their precise meaning. Most of the confusion in the world, he would say, was lack of communication because of the careless use of words so that people rarely understood one another. He decried arguments since they led nowhere because of semantic difficulties. People were using the same words but because of the different connotations each attached to the words he used, there was no meeting of the minds and therefore no real understanding of what they were arguing about. "We are too prone to use words not to illuminate but to persuade", he said, so that such words as good and bad, right and wrong, have little or nothing to tell us about what is good or bad, right or wrong. All that such words describe are the things we like and the things we do not like. When we say a

thing is good, it is because we like it or agree with what it con-
notes for us. When we say it is bad or wrong, we are really
saying that it is something we don't like or don't agree with.
Most of us, unwittingly perhaps, indulge in what Dr. Cronbach
called "propaganda" language and therefore real communication and real dialogue become very difficult to attain.

While at the College I took every course Dr. Cronbach
taught. I often accompanied him on his weekly visits to homes
for the aged, mental hospitals and other institutions for the
poor, the neglected and the forgotten. These visits usually took
place on Saturday afternoon after the morning worship in the
College chapel.

In addition to taking all Dr. Cronbach's courses in social
studies and the psalms, the one I never missed was an extra-
curricular discussion group over which he presided every Saturday morning for an hour and a half before Chapel. Dr. Cronbach was at his desk punctually at 9 a.m. on Saturdays and any
student who cared to drop in was welcome. Sometimes as many
as ten came; often I found myself the only one. It was when we
were alone that I got to know my teacher best and most intimately and was most enriched by his wisdom and by the
sensitivity of his insights. One incident stands out vividly. It was
at one of these informal meetings with about seven students in
the room. The important news of the week for us seminarians
was a story in the *New York Times* about a very successful rabbi
of a large Temple in New York who had decided to leave the
rabbinate because he was frustrated by the small attendance at
Friday evening services. He gave as the reason for his frustration
that he could not compete with the "it" girl, Clara Bow, the
movie sex symbol of the roaring '20s.

The story in the *Times* became the subject of that Saturday
morning's conversation. The question was whether there was a

future for religion in general and for the synagogue in particular since religion and the synagogue could not compete with the distractions of secular entertainment. In the course of the discussion, trying to defend the need for organized religion in spite of the fact that people were abstaining from religious services, I made the statement, "There is no competition in self-effacement". I don't know what I really meant by that statement. Maybe I was trying to say that the rabbi shouldn't try to compete with secular entertainment, that the synagogue was not a playhouse and the service was not a show, that the synagogue had its own role to play, to point up the moral and spiritual ideal whether or not the congregants lived by it, that it was the rabbi's role to express the ideal both by precept and example and not to be frustrated by whether the people followed him or not. Anyway, whatever I was trying to say, Dr. Cronbach took out his little notebook and wrote something in it and tears came to his eyes. I couldn't understand what had happened. The statement seemed to have touched him deeply, but I never knew why until many years later, after I had been a rabbi for 25 years and had gone through some traumatic psychological conflicts myself, that I remembered that morning at the College and I began to understand why Dr. Cronbach was moved to tears by the statement. Self-effacement was for Dr. Cronbach his way of life and unknowingly I had touched the very core of his being.

15
Liverpool, England—My First Congregation

Toward the end of our senior year at Hebrew Union College, my classmates and I, almost ready for ordination, were greatly concerned about our future. We were in the midst of the Great Depression and rumors were streaming in that there would be no congregations for any of us; pulpits that were available were offering wages of less than $2000 a year, some as low as $1100. For a single man it might be a survival wage but for a married man with a child, even $2000 was no living wage. I was already earning more from my editorial work, Sunday school teaching and bi-weekly congregation at Richmond. It was during this time of concern that Miss Sachs, the College president's secretary, came into history class one day with the message that Dr. Morgenstern wanted to see me immediately. Suddenly all the sins I had committed at the College rushed to my consciousness. What had I done to be called into the president's office in the middle of a class?

I left my seat and proceeded with trepidation. Dr. Morgenstern's greeting was brusque but his eyes were smiling. Without asking me to sit down he said, "Raphael, how would you like to go to England?" My first reaction was shock that quickly turned into exhilaration. To go to England, to have an opportunity for a religious experience in a foreign land appealed to my spirit of adventure. My immediate impulse was to say, "Yes, I would like to go to England", then I remembered I was not alone. I was married. I had a wife and year-old daughter. How would Madeline take to the idea of leaving her native land, her family and friends to be a rabbi's wife in a land she knew little about? Dr. Morgenstern didn't make it any easier when he interrupted my thoughts with the further statement that he had to know my
84

decision by the next day and that the position would pay 600 English pounds, in those days about $3000. I mumbled some words of thanks for considering me for the position and said I would let him know the next day. I left the office in a daze and returned to my history class. But my thoughts were not on history. They were full of visions of England and of the opportunity for an unbelievable adventure; above all, there was the wonderful feeling of having an offer of a congregation at a wage which in England was considered quite good for a fledgling rabbi.

I went home still exhilarated but when I told Madeline about the offer, it was her turn to be shocked. Her first reaction was what I had feared, very negative. I spent most of the night trying to convince her of how fortunate we were to have such an offer in these times of economic depression. I explained that congregations were few and that some of my classmates were willing to accept positions at $1500 a year or less. Liverpool was the second best congregation that year; the best offer went to a classmate who was single, as assistant rabbi at Temple Emanu-El, New York. I appealed to Madeline's sense of adventure, to the opportunity of meeting new people—not in a strange land but rather in the motherland of our American culture and tradition and I emphasized how much this experience would mean to my career. Nothing convinced her and I realized I would need more time to come to a decision. I told this to Dr. Morgenstern and he said, "All right. I'll give you till the end of the week—two more days." I was relieved and immensely grateful.

The next two days were full of excitement, what with discussions with Madeline's relatives and one of my professors, Dr. Sheldon Blank, who had lived for a time in England and had married a fine Englishwoman. They encouraged us to accept the position and felt that I would be able to do a really constructive work in strengthening the Liberal Jewish movement which was yet in its infancy in the British Commonwealth. They told me about the kind of people with whom I would be associated: Dr. Israel Mattuck, an American rabbi who had gone to England in 1912 to be the first American Reform rabbi of the budding Liberal Jewish movement founded by Dr. Claude G. Montefiore, a great biblical scholar, and the Hon. Lily Montagu, daughter of Lord Swaythling, for years the head of the Orthodox Jewish community in England. After her father's death the Hon. Lily, with her sister Marion and inspired by Dr. Montefiore, began the Jewish Religious Union to promote a liberal interpretation of Judaism in England.

Under the leadership of Dr. Mattuck, with the support of Dr. Montefiore, and tireless labors of the Hon. Lily, the Liberal movement grew to three congregations: the Liberal Jewish Synagogue of London of which Dr. Mattuck was senior rabbi; another synagogue in North London, and the Liberal Jewish Synagogue in Liverpool which had been organized two years before I came and which was served by Rabbi Morris Goldstein, also an American. It was Rabbi Goldstein's resignation and return to America that prompted Dr. Morgenstern's offer to me of the Liverpool congregation.

Encouraged by Dr. and Mrs. Blank and their reassuring picture of what life in England was like, Madeline finally agreed to accept Dr. Morgenstern's offer. With the decision made, the rest of the school year passed quickly—finishing my thesis, preparing for ordination and making plans for the new life before us.

Ordination in June 1932 was a beautiful, solemn, happy occasion. I was the only graduate to have his baby attend the service. It was a proud day for the Levines. I was now a rabbi, authorized to teach Judaism and be a member of the panel of three judges which constituted a *Beth Din*, a court empowered to hear cases and make decisions according to Jewish law on matters both secular and religious affecting Jewish life.

We spent an exciting summer with my family in Duluth making preparations for England—getting passports, buying clothes, attending farewell parties. About six weeks before the Holyday season was to begin, which in 1932 was on October 1, we left Duluth for New York to board the Corinthia for England.

16
Toward Brotherhood in Liverpool

The Liverpool congregation had a membership of about one hundred. All were formerly associated with one of the largest Orthodox congregations in the Midlands, the Princess Road Synagogue, founded in the 18th century by Jewish immigrants from Germany, Holland and Alsace Lorraine. Rabbi Frampton was its honored and beloved minister and when I came to Liverpool he had already served the congregation for 40 years. Most of those now of my congregation had demanded some religious reforms which Rabbi Frampton was either unwilling or unable to grant. They decided to leave the Princess Road Synagogue and organize their own congregation aided and abetted by Dr. Mattuck and the Hon. Lily Montagu, an indefatigable proselytizer for Liberal Judaism. Rabbi Frampton was unhappy with this wholesale secession but found himself powerless to stop it. I am sure that Rabbi Goldstein, who was the first Reform rabbi of the congregation, must have had a difficult time but by the time I came two years later, the new congregation was fairly well established and more or less accepted. I tried to make friends with Rabbi Frampton. I found him to be a polite English gentleman but the doors to any closer relationship were kept closed.

I was the lone Reform rabbi in Liverpool with the nearest colleague 200 miles away in London. There were other Orthodox congregations in the city but their rabbis were also cool to my gestures of friendship. The clergy most ready to accept me were the Unitarians who had several churches in and around Liverpool. Through several of their ministers with whom I became friends, I joined the Ministers' Association and found the religious fellowship I needed among the Christian clergy. Shortly thereafter I suggested we ought to have occasional meetings outside the formal Association to discuss religious and social problems of concern to all of us as spiritual leaders. I offered our home as a meeting place and Friday evening seemed to be the most convenient time. It was acceptable to me as we had our worship services on Saturday afternoon at 3 o'clock instead of Friday evening as was the custom in America. The 3 o'clock time had been set before I came and the reason, I was told, was to give those who belonged to Orthodox synagogues an opportunity to visit our worship services if they wished, with the hope of winning them over to Liberal Judaism. I continued the practice during my six-year ministry in Liverpool.

After a few evenings of discussion and fellowship with the ministers' group, we decided to formalize our relationship in an organization we called the "World Order Group". In time we were joined by ministers of a number of other denominations including Baptist, Congregational, Methodist and Anglican. Lay people also joined—a writer, teacher, social worker and a young architect, Donald Bradshaw and his wife with whom Madeline and I became intimate friends. The Bradshaws had belonged to the Church of England and had experimented with other denominations, finally deciding on Christian Science. Donald was a highly sensitive, poetic and spiritually oriented young man a few years younger than I. We discovered a deep spiritual kinship with each other and for the last three of my six years in Liverpool, he and his wife never missed our weekly Friday meetings.

The main purpose of our World Order Group was to try to work out programs that would further the cause of peace and good international relations between Britain and the countries of Europe. A number of the ministers considered themselves absolute pacifists and hoped that through the World Order Group, we might exert some influence upon British attitudes, at least in Liverpool. In the middle '30s, the growing menace of Nazism became the major concern of our group and Hitler's virulent anti-Semitism and organized persecution of Jews brought me to the fore as a spokesman for my people. I was inundated with invitations to speak at the churches of World Order Group members to explain what was happening in Germany, and from all kinds of other non-Jewish organizations who couldn't understand why the Jews should be so singled out for persecution by the Nazis.

In 1938 while president of the Liverpool B'nai B'rith, a Jewish fraternal organization, I persuaded members to sponsor a dinner to which each would invite one or more Christian friends as a gesture of fellowship and brotherhood. I was asked to give the toast to our non-Jewish guests and since it represents my present thinking, I would like to quote a part of it here:

> We are living in very troubled times. The number of nations that still retain their political and social sanity is decreasing. In more countries than we like to think, liberty and tolerance and even simple human justice to defenseless minorities—these values which humanity has achieved after so many centuries and at such terrific cost—are being ruthlessly destroyed by an unbridled chauvinism, or are being argued away by a national madness which has become the obsession of rulers and people alike. Democracy and democratic ideals and institutions are being challenged everywhere. We are being told that we are not fit to rule ourselves in freedom, but must be whipped into submission and to blind obedience to the infallible wisdom of a super-

man, the Fuehrer, who is to be the master of our fate and the captain of our soul.

Against this madness there is no greater bulwark in Europe than this country, founded as it is upon the principle which the dictator states are attempting to uproot from European civilization, namely, that the first purpose of a state is to afford its citizens the maximum opportunity for liberty in their personal life, freedom in their spiritual striving, and justice to all regardless of race, creed or color. This principle of government has through centuries of political and social evolution become part of the British heritage. The spiritual values which it has fostered, liberty, and tolerance and fair play, have become woven into the texture of British character, bred in the bone and ingrained in the soul. My country, too, founded by Britons who carried with them across the Atlantic their British heritage, stands in the new world for these self-same ideals. But here in the old world your country stands pre-eminent because of its power and its stability as the champion of democracy and democratic institutions, and as the protagonist of justice and the rights of all men to life, liberty and to freedom to develop their personality in their own way.

Therein lies the source of your power, and your greatness. Because you have learned not merely to tolerate but to respect differences of race and creed, language and culture, you, in your small island, command the loyalties of the most heterogeneous group of peoples ever gathered into one commonwealth of nations. And by that very fact this country stands as the symbol and the promise of that unity which we hope the whole of mankind will ultimately achieve amidst the great diversity of its races and languages, creeds and cultures.

For that is the goal of human striving. The ideal of human brotherhood, which is the cherished hope of us all, does not imply uniformity among men, nor an absence of differences. But it does imply an absence of divisiveness. Differences we want. We would not have it otherwise; for in the diversity of the contributions to civilization lies its rich beauty and its grandeur. After all, whatever beauty and spiritual quality our civilization has achieved has been made possible because there has been a diversity of genius among individuals and among peoples; because there have been Greeks who were gifted with the power to express their soul in beautiful forms; because there have been Romans with a genius for organization and statecraft, and because there have been Hebrews with a passion for God and righteousness which enabled them to give the Bible to the world.

So the world needs its diversity of races and peoples, its languages and cultures, its religions and its differing ways of life—that by their distinctive contributions to humanity each may add a stone to the cathedral of the spirit which the ages are building—the foundation of which is mutual respect and sympathetic understanding and the tower of which is brotherhood.

Tonight we have met to bear witness to this truth. Here we are—Jews and Christians of several denominations— people of different racial backgrounds and differing faiths, yet we are united in fellowship and moved by the deepest sense of good will toward one another because, in spite of our differences, and they are by no means slight, we recognize an overarching unity implicit in our common humanity and in our common desire to further the ideals and

values which all of us cherish, and of which the world today stands in such urgent need.

We are not met for mutual admiration; but for mutual
respect. We have not come to flatter but to try to understand, and above all to bear witness, in these troubled
times, to our faith, in one another and in the future—a
future founded upon truth and justice and the spirit of true
brotherhood.

And so it is with a profound sense of the high significance
of this occasion and conscious of the great privilege be-
stowed upon me that I propose the toast to our guests, our
brethren of other faiths.

The European situation worsened with Hitler's incursions into
the Ruhr and the Rhineland and taking over Austria as a
German satellite. Now he was making demands upon the allies
of World War I, especially France and Britain, for the Sudeten-
land, then under the control of Czechoslovakia, on the pretext
that its population was predominantly German and had belonged to Germany prior to World War I. The British government felt that Hitler had gone too far for continued appease-
ment. But so great was the desire both in France and Britain to
avoid a showdown with Hitler that when Neville Chamberlain,
prime minister of Britain, and Edouard Daladier, premier of
France, went to Munich to discuss the situation with Hitler,
they signed the Munich Pact sacrificing Czechoslovakia's interests for what they hoped would be the last of Hitler's demands.

The night before the Munich Pact was signed, in October
1938, our World Order Group met to discuss what to do in the
event Chamberlain failed in his mission, and war with Nazi

Germany could not be avoided. The whole of that day was tense with activity and rumor. War seemed imminent. Britain had mobilized its fleet. A blackout was ordered throughout the country and gas masks were issued in preparation for possible war. The question before our group was whether if war came we would in the spirit of our pacifist leanings refuse to participate and if necessary claim conscientious objection to any military activity. The absolute pacifists among us said they had no choice. They would under no circumstances do anything to help Britain's war effort should she become involved. I took issue with my friends and tried to convince them that this was not a situation where absolute pacifist principles could be invoked.

Justified as I felt as a Jew to do everything in my power to destroy Nazism—and I admitted my bias—my reasons for participation if war came were moral, not personal. I agreed with the absolute pacifists that moral ends cannot justify immoral means, that moral persuasion is infinitely superior to the use of force to achieve moral ends. However, in order for moral persuasion to operate, there must be a moral conscience to which a moral appeal can be made. In the situation which confronted us at the moment, there was no conscience in any sense that our Judaeo-Christian tradition recognized as moral in Hitler and Nazism to which any moral appeal we might make could or would be understood or accepted. On the contrary, Hitler rejected every aspect of the Judaeo-Christian value system as the morality of slaves, to be rejected and destroyed by the German Herrenfolk, the master race destined to rule the world. To submit to such an evil was in my judgment not only un-Jewish but also un-Christian.

No one really knows what Jesus meant when he said, "You have heard that it is said, 'an eye for an eye and a tooth for a tooth', but I say unto you, do not resist one who is evil. If any-one strikes you on the right cheek, turn to him the other also." If he meant, as I believe he did and as many Christian thinkers interpret this non-resistance doctrine to mean, that one must not return evil for evil, blow for blow, insult for insult, but should return good for the evil done him in the hope that this might soften the evildoer, make him contrite and inspire him to turn from his evil ways, then the non-resistance doctrine has a rational, spiritual and psychological validity. This kind of moral power can and often has transformed evildoers into saints. But Hitler and the Nazis had rejected such spiritual power as the weakness of slaves. They relied entirely on the power of the mailed fist. The only way other than complete surrender to an evil such as this was to resist it with every means available to us. So we argued until dawn not knowing whether or not we would have to put our philosophies to the test the next day.

In the morning we got the news that Neville Chamberlain was on his way home with the Munich Pact signed, rejoicing in his assurance that we had achieved "peace in our time". The world was to rue the consequence of the Munich Pact. But that we did not know on the day of reprieve from imminent war, October 1, 1938.

17
London and the Blitz

After six years in Liverpool, I received a call to the mother Liberal Jewish synagogue in the St. John's Wood district of London with a congregation of more than 1500.

When Donald Bradshaw and his wife heard the news of our impending departure, they came to our home one night and told me they had decided to convert to Judaism. I was not greatly surprised. During the years of the World Order Group, they had been the most ardent and loyal members and were our closest non-Jewish friends. My first question was, "Why? Why do you want to become Jews?" Donald reminded me that they had been coming to the Friday evening meetings for three years; he said they had come to realize that Judaism was the kind of religion they were looking for.

I pointed out that in discussing Judaism at these meetings, we had concentrated on its ideal aspects, its prophetic tradition, its moral and spiritual values, but that not all Jews were prophets or idealists. They were people with human weaknesses, common to all. I asked the Bradshaws to reflect on what they would gain —would they be better by changing their label from Christian to Jew; would they have deeper insights than they already had or greater sensitivity? I reminded them that they knew very few Jews personally and that becoming a Jew is more than accepting a creed or theology. It is identification with an historic, ethnic group, a people with a unique experience to which they would always be strangers. Nor is the synagogue merely a religious institution, I said. It is also a social center for the Jewish community. I told the Bradshaws I would not encourage them to think of any kind of formal conversion to Judaism.

Twenty years later on a sabbatical leave from my congregation in Seattle, I visited Liverpool and called Donald Bradshaw
who was then a professor of architecture at the University of
Liverpool. He told me how grateful he and his wife were that
I had not accepted them into Judaism when they asked me to.
They had gone back to the Church of England; he was a
deacon in that Church and both were teachers in the religion
school and happy in having rediscovered the religion which was
their heritage.

It has always been my conviction that there are two kinds of
religion, *institutional* which is sectarian and represents the cultural heritage of the individual born into a particular religious
group and his identification with the group, and *personal* religion which is the individual's personal commitment to God,
the Father of us all. The personal commitment to God is witnessed not by the kind of church a person belongs to but the life
he lives which every great religion describes in terms of man's
loving relationship with God and with his brother man.

Shortly after I became an associate rabbi of the London congregation, the effect of the Nuremberg laws to dehumanize the
Jews in Germany began to be felt in the stream of emigres from
Germany who flooded London on their way to lands of refuge
in Ireland, Africa, Australia, South America, Mexico, the
United States and wherever else they could find an escape from
Nazi persecution. I was assigned the duty of helping emigres
who had belonged to non-Orthodox synagogues in Germany. I
organized the Friendship Club where emigres could meet at the
synagogue for social contacts and attend classes in English with
volunteer teachers from the congregation. Eventually the Club
had more than a thousand members, among them some rabbis
who had managed to escape from Germany. To make their so-
journ in London a little easier, we helped them to organize into

a community of their own under the leadership of their own rabbis and gave them synagogue facilities to carry on their own program. In this way we tried to help these refugees begin anew in England or to endure their exile more easily while they awaited visas and transportation to countries willing to receive them.

By 1939 the European situation was becoming increasingly tense. The Munich Pact gave Hitler time to consolidate his gains. Having swallowed up Czechoslovakia, he now began to make demands on Poland. Britain and France issued a warning to Hitler that any aggression against Polish independence would trigger a European war. Hitler concluded a firm military alliance with Mussolini and three months later, a ten-year non-aggression and neutrality pact with Soviet Russia. Having secured his eastern borders, he struck at Poland with lightning rapidity which foreshadowed the "blitz" technique he was prepared to use.

As I watched the rapidly deteriorating situation, I did not want my family, now with two children, Lori Jean, who was nearly eight, and David, eight months and retarded from birth, to stay in England. I persuaded Madeline to take the children on a vacation to America. If war came they would remain there; if not they could return. Within a few weeks Britain and France were at war with Germany. The synagogue, situated in the heart of London, was vulnerable to air attack since a block behind it was the important Marylebone electric power station, a prime target. However, the synagogue was the most solid brick structure within a radius of half a mile and had a large basement area suitable as an air raid shelter into which it was converted.

After Madeline and the children left, I went to live in the home of an elderly couple—the Goldsteins. The aerial blitz began with daylight attacks which were repulsed by the Spit-fires. So nightly ·raids began and continued for more than a year. Military targets were no longer singled out for attack. Bombing became indiscriminate. Every morning we would hear of civilian casualties caught in their homes and often in the air raid shelters they had built in their gardens or in some of the public shelters to which they went at night for safety. So often people in shelters were killed while their homes escaped direct hits that many began to take a fatalistic attitude toward the bombing. It seemed useless to hide.

People in London tried to carry on during the blitz as normal-ly as possible. During the day they were fairly safe from attack. At dusk everybody prepared for the air raids. Entire families flocked to shelters before dark and every platform and tunnel of the subway was strewn with sleeping forms. One night when I was working in my study at the synagogue later than usual, I decided to spend the night in the air raid shelter. About mid-night the wardens came in and ordered everyone to evacuate the basement of the synagogue. A bomb had landed in front of the building and it was not known if it was a dud or a delayed action bomb. I chose to go to an old Episcopal Church about a half mile from the synagogue which also had a shelter in its basement. When the all clear sounded I went into the city for food and saw along the three-mile route some of the havoc which the night's raid had wrought. Most of the buildings were intact except for glass that was strewn through the streets. In town the crowds were already gathered discussing the raid and filling the tea shops that were open. There was no panic or dis-order. The people had become so accustomed to these night raids that the raids became a part of their way of life.

After another raid, as I was walking from the Goldstein apartment to the synagogue, I passed a number of shops that had been almost completely demolished. The owner of one had collected the canned goods and groceries he was able to salvage and had piled them neatly in front of his demolished shop. A sign on top of the heap read: "My shop is more open than usual".

I arrived at the synagogue to see a huge crowd gathered; there had been a direct hit. No one in the basement shelter had been injured but my study was in the direct path of the bomb and my books and papers lay with the rubble in the crater below. The main sanctuary had been partially destroyed and gutted and most of the rest of the building was unusable. Several of the ministers of nearby churches, both Catholic and Protestant, offered their buildings for Jewish worship and gatherings. The rabbis accepted the offer of Lords Cricket Club across the street from the synagogue which had a large hall that could be used for worship and for almost a year the Cricket Club served as synagogue.

18 Return to America

As the war progressed and the blitz failed to cow Britain into submission, as Hitler invaded Russia despite the non-aggression pact, it looked as if the war would drag on indefinitely and I began thinking about returning to America. It had been more than two years since I had seen Madeline and the children. Madeline had made it clear that she would not return to England. I had stayed with the congregation during the entire blitz and hard as it was to leave them, they understood my decision and gave me their blessing.

Travel arrangements were difficult. Because of the menace of Nazi indiscriminate U-boat warfare on all shipping leaving Britain, the American Embassy strongly urged American citizens to travel by air. Besides, if I could arrive in time to take part in the High Holyday services, it would greatly facilitate my getting a new assignment. Things went well in the beginning and by the time my papers were ready I was able to get a flight to Lisbon where I could board a clipper ship for New York. But engine trouble forced an 11-day stop-over in Ireland. I missed the clipper ship in Lisbon and had no money to see me through a two-week wait for the next one. So I exchanged my air ticket for passage on an American Export Lines ship and faced the U-boat hazards.

On arrival I wired Ida, now living in Minneapolis, that I was in New York without funds and she wired me the fare to Minneapolis. On the way I stopped to see Dr. Morgenstern, still president of Hebrew Union College, to whom I had written about a Holyday position. The letter had never arrived but it would not have helped anyway because of the delay. It was now the second day of Rosh Hashanah. Dr. Morgenstern did promise to recommend me for one of the several congregations that were sure to be opening during the year and with that assurance I went on to Minneapolis and then to Portland for a reunion with Madeline and Lori Jean, then living with Madeline's youngest sister. David had been left in Cincinnati in the care of a motherly woman who worked with handicapped children. Later he was moved to the Washington State Custodial School for the Mentally Retarded where he died at the age of 20.

While in Portland I was invited to speak in the Reform synagogue and the Portland City Club about my experiences as a rabbi in London during the blitz. One who heard me was David Robinson, Western Regional Director of B'nai B'rith, who put me in touch with Richard Gudstadt, then head of the Anti-Defamation League in Chicago. It was a time for growing anti-Semitism in America and just a month before Pearl Harbor, and both Mr. Robinson and Mr. Gudstadt thought I should share my experiences and insights concerning the war on a lecture tour of the United States.

Just before the lecture tour was to begin, I received a letter from Dr. Morgenstern informing me that Rabbi Samuel Koch of the Temple De Hirsch in Seattle was retiring and the pulpit committee of the Temple was seeking a successor. He was recommending me, along with five others, for the position. There was also an opening in Lexington, Kentucky and the congregation there would contact me. I was elated. There was no place I wanted more to serve as a rabbi than in Seattle. Madeline had never ceased to extol the wondrous beauty of the Pacific Northwest and especially Seattle. On my one visit there to give a lecture a few weeks earlier, I found it to be all she said it was.

Many months passed before I heard anything at all from Seattle. The Lexington congregation invited me to visit them and I spent two days meeting leading members of the congregation individually and at evening gatherings. Later, while on the lecture tour, I received a letter from them thanking me for my interest but that after considerable discussion they felt that with my experience, I would not remain long in such a small congregation. Their rejection proved a blessing as with so many other frustrated expectations in life.

After the attack on Pearl Harbor, "I Saw London Bombed" took on new urgency, especially in a coastal city like Seattle with all its prime targets. I still had heard nothing from the Temple De Hirsch congregation when I spoke to about 400 businessmen at a Chamber of Commerce meeting. I told of my experiences during the blitz as a fire watcher and air raid worker, trying to give them some idea of the wonderful spirit of the British during their darkest hour. Immediately after the meeting, the chief of the local civil defense asked if I would stay over till the following Monday to address about 2000 police and defense workers at the Civic Auditorium.

The congregation had not yet selected a successor to Rabbi Koch and the reception I got at the Chamber of Commerce meeting impressed members of the Temple Board of Trustees. The next morning I received a call from the chairman of the pulpit committee asking if I was still interested; I was the only candidate now being considered. That Friday evening I conducted the service and gave a sermon tying it in with Passover being celebrated that week with its ideals of freedom, using some of my experiences in London as illustrations of faith in freedom and the willingness to make great sacrifices to preserve it against tyrants who would destroy it.

Within eight days I was elected rabbi of the congregation—as I often said later, half in jest and half in earnest, by the Seattle Chamber of Commerce. My fondest dream had been realized. I was to be rabbi of the one congregation in America that would have been my first choice had I been given the choice. Madeline was supremely happy. I would begin my official duties on June 4, 1942.

My first years in Seattle were very exciting. My honeymoon with the congregation lasted much longer than I had dared hope for. New members came in large numbers so that the congregation grew from 400 to nearly a thousand in ten years and our religion school grew in proportion. I was very active in the Christian community, encouraged both by my congregation in my efforts to build bridges of understanding and by our Christian neighbors' response. I found that seven days a week was hardly enough to do all the things with which I became involved, unfortunately to the neglect of my family. This became a source of tension between Madeline and me, which with other personal problems, led to a deterioration of our relationship and ultimately to a separation in 1953 after nearly 25 years of marriage. It was a traumatic experience for both of us, but at the time it seemed the only way of avoiding even more harmful results.

For six years I lived alone, determined never to marry again because it would be unfair to any woman, married as I was to my work. Then I met Reeva Miller when she was resident arts and craft teacher at the Camp for Living Judaism in the Santa Cruz mountains near Saratoga, California. I was there as rabbi-counselor and in the process of writing a book. I needed someone to do some art work for the book and Reeva volunteered to do it. We became friends and I used to see her occasionally when I visited Ida who was now living on a cattle feeding ranch in El Centro, California, which she and her husband operated. In 1958 on one of my winter vacations at the ranch, I found Reeva there. She and my sister had been friends for years and she occasionally visited El Centro, especially when she was having difficulties at home. Her marriage had been unhappy almost from the beginning. She and her husband had been divorced once but had later reconciled. Now they were again in the process of getting a divorce, this time irrevocable, and Reeva had come to El Centro for help and encouragement. When her divorce became final, we decided to get married.

19
Religious Camping

I had been rabbi of Temple De Hirsch about a year when I received an invitation from the National Conference of Christians and Jews to be a counselor for a week at a Christian religious camp at Seabeck on Hoods Canal. I had never been to any kind of religious camp before. The group was composed of 200 high school students, boys and girls, from all over the state of Washington. It was a joint venture of two denominations, Baptist and Disciples of Christ churches. My assignment was to teach a course in "Building Bridges of Understanding" carrying the brotherhood message which was the NCCJ's basic reason for existence and activity.

To help me in my assignment, the NCCJ gave me a list of 20 questions which I was to put to my class to determine their attitudes toward people of ethnic and religious groups other than their own. The questions were related to their attitudes toward Catholics, Jews and Negroes—whether they would approve or disapprove having one of these minority groups as a member of their athletic teams or social groups; as a teacher or personal friend; whether they would invite one to their homes; elect one as a representative in government or join in any other association involving closer relations with any of them. The answers were to be unsigned.

I gave my class of 25 this questionnaire at our first meeting. The answers did not surprise me. The negative answers to most of the questions were high, about 60% against Catholics, 75% against Jews, 90% against Negroes. I did not tell the class the results of the survey. That week I conducted my class in human relations trying to give them some understanding of how people needed to learn to get along with others in spite of their dif-
106

ferences of race, color or religious faith not only for the welfare of our country made up of all these diverse groups but for their own growth as human beings. I conducted my class informally and tried to help the young people understand the problems of human relations through probing their own attitudes and experiences in a free and open discussion. To work in this way was a new experience for me and one I greatly enjoyed. But more important than the class experience was living with the campers and their counselors, ministers and Sunday school teachers and participating in the program from the early morning watch to the closing friendship circle at night. I was deeply moved by what I saw accomplished as the days went by until toward the end of the week we felt like one united family with a common purpose.

At the end of the week I gave my class the same questionnaire as at the first session to see if their attitudes had changed as a result of the week's experience. No names were to be signed. The answers this time were a surprise. The negative responses against Catholics decreased from 60% to 15%; against Negroes, from 90% to 40%; against Jews, not a single negative answer. These young people were all white Protestant, mostly from small communities where ethnic minorities were rare. Few of them had ever had any personal contact with Jews and hardly any with Negroes or Catholics.

This experience in trying to build bridges of understanding between people convinced me that the best way to combat prejudice was not by preaching brotherhood or lecturing on human relations but by creating the environment in which people of diverse racial and religious backgrounds can meet and work together on equal terms for a common purpose. The camp offered that kind of environment. There was nothing quite like it in any branch of Judaism. This I decided we Jews must have.

How to accomplish it I did not know but it had to be if we were ever to inspire our Jewish youth with loyalty to their faith and their synagogue. At that time there was hardly a synagogue in the country that had any effective program for young people after they were confirmed at 15.

In 1945 I attended a rabbinical conference in Cincinnati and one day called all my colleagues from Pacific Coast states together for a breakfast meeting. At the meeting I suggested it would be helpful for all of us on the Pacific Coast, far from the mainstream of our Reform movement, to organize some kind of association to meet perhaps once a year for discussion of subjects of mutual interest and for fellowship. Isolated as I was in the Northwest with my nearest colleague in Portland, I keenly felt this loneliness.

The following January ten of us met in San Francisco and formed the Western Association of Reform Rabbis. In January 1947 we held our first full conference at Los Angeles and to the original ten at the organization meeting were added another 15 from Los Angeles and Southern California and their wives. The agenda dealt largely with purposes and goals of our association and programs to implement these goals. During the meetings I told my colleagues of my experience at the Christian youth camp and suggested that our organization undertake as its first project a religious co-educational camping program for our high school juniors and seniors, and perhaps freshmen in college.

The suggestion was received without enthusiasm. There were many who argued that it would never work, that we were not ready for such an undertaking and besides, Jewish youth would not go for a religious camp. "How do you know they wouldn't? Have we ever given them a chance?" I challenged. Rabbi Iser Freund of San Jose had also been a counselor at a Christian camp and enthusiastically supported the idea. I volunteered to organize such a camp if someone would find a suitable site. Rabbi Freund volunteered to find such a place. With these two offers, Association members reluctantly voted to let us go ahead.

I could hardly wait to return to Seattle to inform our Temple Board of Trustees and the boards of the Temple Brotherhood and Sisterhood about the camping program. My enthusiasm was contagious and they promised to help. Rabbi Freund immediately contacted Rev. Peabody, a Christian friend who was associated with a camp at Lake Tahoe, and was able to obtain the Presbyterian conference grounds at Zephyr Cove for our group at a cost of $18 a week for room and meals provided we had 100 campers.

At first young people were dubious about the attractiveness of a religious camp, but the prospect of going to California and meeting boys and girls their own age from other states was alluring enough to overcome doubts. We distributed 20 camperships among the most promising students of our youth group and these persuaded 20 more to sign up for the program. It was more difficult to interest young people in other areas because of the lack of interest among rabbis, but we finally had 94, six short of the required 100. By counting faculty and their wives we managed to more than fill the quota.

The week's program was a duplicate of the memorable week I had spent at Seabeck, only the content was Jewish. From the waking bell at 7 a.m. to the friendship circle at 10:30 p.m., the day was filled with worship, study, recreation and special interest groups. The climax of the week was the Sabbath worship. We contacted the small Jewish community in Reno, Nevada, and they lent us a Torah, necessary for Scripture reading, and with the Torah came a delegation of their leaders to see what we were doing at a Presbyterian camp. As the service progressed, few eyes were dry under the emotional impact of worship conducted entirely by the young people with the exception of the Torah reading and sermon.

For the second Jewish youth conference there was no difficulty in getting rabbis and campers interested. By the fourth year we had to establish quotas for participating congregations, so great was the demand. During the year Mr. Ben Swig, a San Francisco philanthropist, was brought by his rabbi to the YWCA conference grounds near Carmel, California, where the camp was then held to see what we were doing. Mr. Swig was deeply impressed and seeing the potential for religious camping, he decided that we could no longer be dependent on rented facilities. He found a 200-acre estate in the Santa Cruz mountains near Saratoga, California, and in 1951 Camp Saratoga, the Camp for Living Judaism, was dedicated as the first religious camp in the Reform movement. Today there are nine regional camps throughout the country operated by the Union of American Hebrew Congregations, the national body of Reform Judaism. They have revitalized our youth movement and have become the source of inspiration to many young men and women now being recruited for the rabbinate, religious education and lay leadership.

20
Launching of "Challenge"

It was in 1960 when John Fitzgerald Kennedy was nominated for the presidency of the U.S. that I began to receive a rash of hate mail against the possibility of a Catholic president. It reminded me of what happened when another Catholic, Alfred Smith, three-time governor of New York, was nominated in 1928. While many factors defeated Al Smith, not the least of them was the widespread bigotry against Catholics which swept the country. It was after that that Charles Evans Hughes, then Chief Justice of the Supreme Court, along with several friends who were aware of the religious bigotry, decided to do something about it. They organized what later became the National Conference of Christians and Jews to help the American people realize the necessity for religious tolerance and understanding as the basis for survival not only of religion in America, but of America itself.

For some time before Kennedy's nomination I had been interested in organizing some type of TV program in Seattle which would include a Protestant, a Catholic and a Jew to help break down some of the religious barriers which had been dividing people across the centuries into mutually exclusive and often hostile groups. Religion, which I was convinced was intended by God to be a healing balm, uniting mankind in the spirit of love and brotherhood, had become one of its most divisive forces, certainly in the last 1900 years. The religious wars during the Middle Ages, and even into our own time, were to me a blasphemy against the God of love whom the belligerent religionists claimed to worship. In the name of this God of love they slaughtered each other with a viciousness unparalleled until the Nazis came with their extermination camps.

111

I had come to feel that the sectarian faiths of organized religion were an evil in the divisive character that grew out of their imperialistic claims to unique religious revelations and infallible truth. Out of this came the need to proselytize by preaching and often by force as the holy wars of the Moslems, the crusades of the Christians, the wars of the Reformation and the extirpation of heresies evidenced so tragically through the centuries.

At one time in my rabbinate, disgusted with this kind of divisiveness, I even considered the idea of organizing some kind of universal religion. Fortunately I came to my senses, realizing that even if I were successful, I would only add another sect to the many already in existence. Instead I decided to concentrate on trying to build bridges of understanding, especially between Christians and Jews.

My motivation grew out of the fact that as Jews we were particularly vulnerable and the chief victims of religious prejudice. Living as we do in countries predominantly Christian, the need for understanding the basic unity between Christianity and Judaism in their moral value systems and ethical ideals was vital to our Jewish survival and the only hope for peaceful co-existence with our Christian neighbors.

When I came to Seattle in 1942, anti-Semitism was virulent and widespread in this country. The "Silver Shirts", Father Coughlin's radio program with his insinuations and open attacks on Jews and Judaism, and Gerald K. Smith with his hate campaign against Catholics, Blacks and Jews, made the need for better understanding between Christians and Jews urgent.

I welcomed every opportunity to speak in churches and before Christian groups. I joined the local chapter of the National Conference of Christians and Jews which at that time had lost the confidence of the Catholic Bishop of Seattle, Gerald

Shaughnessy, so that he had withdrawn Catholic support from the organization. I went to see him but he felt that the NCCJ with its three-faith program only confused the faithful and would lead to religious indifferentism.

Having no success with Bishop Shaughnessy I had to work within the Protestant community and there I found a warm response from the leaders of the major denominations. One of the relationships I cherished was with the late Stephan Bayne, Jr., Bishop of the Episcopal Diocese of Olympia. He came to Seattle in 1946 and I was invited to participate in his investiture. We became close friends and in the dialogues we frequently had, our faith in the ability of Christians and Jews to enrich one another grew firmer.

To break down barriers and to build bridges of understanding between all faiths, but especially between Christians and Jews, became the dominant thrust of my ministry. In 1952 I suggested to Bishop Bayne the possibility of a TV program and told him I would speak to the Catholic Bishop, the Most Reverend Thomas A. Connolly. Bishop Bayne was enthusiastic about the possibilities for such a program. Bishop Connolly was not. The idea died because the station willing to sponsor such a program was not interested without a Catholic participant.

In 1960 when it looked as if we might have another age of bigotry in America, I again went to Bishop Connolly, now Archbishop, and suggested that at least in Seattle and wherever our influence might reach we would try to avoid the repetition of what happened in the election campaign of 1928. Archbishop Connolly was cool to the proposition. He did not believe that it would be effective or that it would last. However, he agreed to think about it and discuss it with some of his advisers. Several weeks went by and I heard nothing. One night I called him and asked whether he had considered the television program because this time we had a station, KOMO-TV, willing to give us excellent time if we could arrange to have the three faiths participate. The Archbishop said he had thought about it but had not yet come to a decision and would let me know within a week.

I did not even remember having met Father Treacy outside the Archbishop's office when I received a call from him saying that the Archbishop wanted him to see me to discuss the possibility of the television program the Archbishop and I had talked about. I was overjoyed.

When Father Treacy came into my study at the Temple my heart sank. I saw a boyish young man who looked in his mid-twenties, although I later discovered he was past 40, and I wondered if the Archbishop was really serious about the program, sending a boy to do a man's work. How could he send a priest so young and immature to represent the Catholic Church on a television program whose other two members were Dr. Martin Goslin of the largest Congregational Church in Seattle and one of the most prominent ministers in the Northwest, and I who had some stature among rabbis? Anyway, since Father Treacy was chosen as the representative, I resolved to work with him as best I could. We discussed the ground rules on which the program was to be established. There were to be no arguments on theology. There was to be no baiting of one another. The important thing was to discuss those things that our three religious faiths had in common and try to build a better understanding between them. These were ground rules that I had already discussed with the Archbishop because neither did I want religious arguments. I wanted discussion. I wanted dialogue. I did not want arguments. I realized that one cannot argue fruitfully about faith. All we can do is try to understand, not merely with tolerance but respect, the other person's point of view, whether we agree with it or not.

Father Treacy began fearful of how he would fare in a discussion with a Protestant and a Jew. He was guarded in his comments. He did his homework thoroughly. He was clearly on the defensive. In a way, we all were on the defensive against each other, trying to protect our faith against any possible implication that the others might have something ours did not have. We soon realized that the purpose of the program was not to win debating points for our own faith but to try to understand each other and our respective faiths.

As the weeks went by and Father Treacy began to feel that we were indeed his friends and colleagues in a common effort toward mutual understanding and good will, his self-confidence grew and we were able to discuss almost anything, no matter how delicate or controversial, with a sensitivity and respect which became the hallmark of CHALLENGE. So on Palm Sunday of the first year of CHALLENGE, we telecast a most delicate discussion, especially between Christians and Jews at that time of the year: "Who Crucified Jesus?"

In 1962 the National Conference of Christians and Jews, influenced especially by this program, presented CHALLENGE with a special national award and in announcing the award at the annual brotherhood dinner of the Washington region, the director said: "It has been the policy of the National Conference of Christians and Jews to select non-clergy to receive awards at the annual brotherhood dinner. However, the service of the CHALLENGE panel is so unique and has had such an impact on the community that the committee felt it must recognize this outstanding contribution to brotherhood; therefore this special award is presented to Rabbi Raphael Levine, Dr. Martin Goslin and Father William Treacy."

As I grew to know Father Treacy more intimately as a person and as a friend, I discovered the great gifts that were his all along and saw him grow in his freedom to use them. His spirit revealed him to be a true disciple of Pope John and led me to apologize on many occasions about how mistaken I was about him at our first meeting. Far from the Archbishop not respecting the television project in sending such a young priest, as I then thought, he had demonstrated great wisdom and understanding when he selected this chancery assistant for so important a mission. Father Treacy had not only the intellectual capacity but he possessed the qualities of heart and spirit to be a most worthy representative of the Church in this stage of the Church's history.

The years of CHALLENGE continued and my relationship with Father Treacy became closer and deeper until I felt toward him as though he were my son and he regarded me as a spiritual father. An eloquent expression of this relationship and the love we felt for each other came when Vatican Council II decreed that at the celebration of Mass the priest should face the congregation rather than stand at the altar with his back to them.

One day Father Treacy came to me and said, "Rabbi, you once promised to make me something if I ever had a parish of my own". My hobby, as he knew, was working in wood and mosaic in the basement of my home. I had made a number of tables, mostly with a chessboard center, on which I had carved some of my favorite quotations. When he asked me to make him something, I thought it was something like a plaque for his study. He reminded me that Mass was now to be celebrated with the priest facing the people. And then he said, "The altar at St. Patrick's is of marble and attached to the wall. It can't be moved. I need a new altar and I must have it within ten days." I was flabbergasted. I knew that the altar was the focal point of Catholic worship, the holiest object in the church, and that he should ask me, a Jew and a rabbi, to make an altar for him touched me deeply. I went to work doing some research on what an altar was and discovered that the least one could use in a church the size of St. Patrick's was a six-foot table.

I worked day and night. The result was an altar of mahogany, birch and walnut. With the help of Reeva, I put on the altar all the symbols that Father Treacy wanted and which meant so much to him, the Chi-Rho in mosaic tile on the center front, and on an ornamental facade at the top, lilies and fish which are ancient Christian symbols.

The altar was completed on the day before it was to be used. Members of his parish carted it to the church and put it in place. A newspaperman from The Seattle Times heard about the altar and decided to do a feature story for the Sunday edition on the day it was to be dedicated and the first Mass in the new form celebrated. The wire news services picked up the story and it was carried in newspapers throughout the United States and beyond. We began to receive letters from all over the world. The response to our simple expression of respect and love was heart-warming and indicated release of something also very deep in other hearts.

It appeared that the impact of this incident touched the lives of many and awakened a hope and a faith that at long last religion which had divided our human family into mutually exclusive and so often antagonistic sectarian groups might bring them together to a spiritual unity as children of God. For had not the Hebrew Prophet Malachi said, perhaps 2500 years ago: "Have we not all one Father? Hath not one God created us all? Why then do we deal treacherously, brother against brother?" (Malachi 2:15) And did not Jesus quote the injunctions from the Old Testament books of Leviticus and Deuteronomy when he said: "You shall love the Lord your God with all your heart, with all your soul, with all your strength and with all your mind. This is the first and greatest commandment, and the second is like unto it, you shall love your neighbor as yourself"? (Luke 10:27) And Paul added: "On these two commandments hang all the Law (Torah) and the prophets". (Gal. 5:14) How can we show our love of God except as we show love for our fellowman?

I tell the story of the altar to demonstrate the closeness of the relationship which Father Treacy and I had established so that he would not hesitate to ask his friend, the Rabbi, to make for him the holiest religious object in the Roman Catholic Church. On my part there was no hesitation to do this for him, even though some of my colleagues in the rabbinate thought that it was not the kind of object a rabbi should make even for his dearest Catholic friend.

As our friendship grew and deepened we achieved a depth of communication rare even between the best of friends. A severe test of our friendship came when the highly emotional issue of liberalizing our state's abortion laws was being debated by the state legislature. Emotions ran deep between those opposing any attempt to make it easier to terminate unwanted pregnancies and those urging reform in the law.

In spite of the danger of discussing this controversial issue on CHALLENGE we decided that we had a responsibility as leaders of our faiths to put the issue before the public as fairly and as honestly as we could. Father Treacy expressed the position of the Roman Catholic Church and his own on the question eloquently and with a frankness and sincerity that was obvious but also with respect and sensitivity to the attitudes of those like Dr. Corson and myself who held equally deep, equally sincere, but different convictions on the issue, although ours did not represent the views of all Jews and Protestants.

We made two programs on this subject and received many letters, some condemning us for being too tolerant of each other, some disappointed that we could disagree so sharply. So we felt the need for doing a third program which we called "The Spirit of CHALLENGE—The Need to Learn How to Disagree Agreeably", a need we believed belonged to the very essence of true religion and the very foundation of any free, democratic society.

Whether or not we got through to our critics we never knew, but I am confident that fair-minded people obtained a better understanding after this third program of how it is possible, even inevitable, for a religious and deeply committed person to have deep convictions on fundamental issues, especially where faith is concerned, and yet have respect for the different and even opposing convictions held by other people. Father Treacy and I share the opinion that this is religion at its truest and best, and certainly the basis of democracy.

21
From Fear to Brotherhood

Long before I met Father Treacy my spiritual odyssey from fear to understanding and appreciation of Christianity as revealed in the life and teachings of Jesus, were gradual steps beginning with the love I had for Miss Calverly, the principal of my first grammar school in Duluth who "mothered" me as a child of eight in my difficult period of becoming Americanized. From her and from some of my early non-Jewish teachers and classmates, I began to learn that there were different kinds of Christians, some good and some bad. This knowledge grew as I came to a more mature understanding of my own religion and other faiths. I began to realize how unjust, unfair and even unintelligent it was to judge religions by any personal experience with only their inadequate representatives or by some of their beliefs and practices which because of my ignorance seemed to me foolish, superstitious, incredible or barbaric.

Dr. Abraham Cronbach, my beloved teacher at Hebrew Union College, helped me more than any other person in that growing understanding of my own religion and other faiths. He taught me how to free myself from stereotype thinking and conditioning, to keep a mind open to new ideas, to suspend judgment upon things that I did not fully comprehend, and above all to guard against generalizing from insufficient experience. The injunction of Rabbi Hillel, who was the spiritual leader of the Jews in Judea when Jesus was but a child, made a profound impression upon me: "Pass not judgment upon your neighbor until you are come into his place", until you yourself have experienced his situation. That insight into the need for empathy was deepened for me by what I learned from Dr.

120

Cronbach and what my personal experience in all the years since has taught me.

This insight, certainly in relation to Christians, grew in my experience as a rabbi in Liverpool. I discovered that the spirit of love and brotherhood which was Judaism as I had come to know it and to expect from Jews, certainly from rabbis, was not practiced toward me nearly so generously by my Orthodox rabbinic colleagues as by some Christian ministers with whom I shared an enriching friendship. I was not angry because my Orthodox colleagues rejected my attempts at friendship with them. I understood their position. I was in their opinion a heretic, a betrayer of Judaism. I did not condemn them, nor did I condemn Orthodox Judaism. I had known Orthodox rabbis in my time and many Orthodox Jewish men and women who were saintly, generous, kind and great-hearted. They were the products of the same Judaism that I had come from. But I became ever more convinced of the need to judge a religion not merely by representatives who were limited by their own personal inadequacies but more by those who tried to witness by their lives the essential idealism and beauty of their faith.

As I studied the Scriptures of other religions, I was amazed at how similar they were, in so many ways, to the ideals and values Judaism proclaimed as man's way to God. I discovered that in all the great religions, and especially in the teachings of Jesus, the door to God could be opened only with the key of love. As a Jew, I had learned from the commandments "to love God with heart and soul and might" and this I recited every day in the Sh'mah—the watchword of my faith (Deut. 6)—and "to love my neighbor as myself", which the holiness code in the book of Leviticus taught me is the way to that love of God. The holiness code I learned is also basic to Christianity, to Islam, to Buddhism, and to other of the great world religions. They expressed it in different idioms and dramatized it in different symbols and forms of worship, but it is practiced with the same varying degree of devotion by their followers as among my own fellow Jews.

These discoveries I made as I followed my beloved teacher's advice to free myself from stereotype thinking about other religions and peoples, to keep a mind open to truth wherever I was able to find it, to free myself as much as possible from the natural human tendency to rationalize my prejudices and call it honest, rational thinking and behavior; and the journey from my childhood fear of Christians and Christianity to a reverent respect for the faith of the Christian friends whom I had grown to love as fellow human beings was fairly uncomplicated.

So when I met Father Treacy, I was ready for the kind of relationship we established across the past 14 years and which we are trying to describe in this book. In Father Treacy's description of how our relationship influenced his life, deepened his insight into his faith as a Catholic and enriched his ministry to his people, he gave undue credit to my part in his spiritual growth. It is true that I may have helped to open windows for him through our CHALLENGE program and through our growing personal friendship. After all, I am 20 years older than he and my experiences have been more varied, but if I claim any credit at all, it was to help him release some of the great potentials of mind and heart and spirit with which God had endowed him from birth.

These potentials and qualities of character he had developed long before I knew him, which he revealed to me almost from the first CHALLENGE program in 1960 and which became clearer and more precious to me as I grew to know him across the years, became a source of strength and enrichment to me.

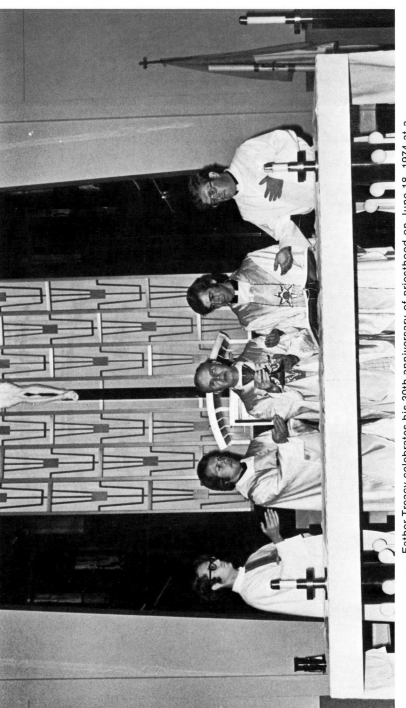

Father Treacy celebrates his 30th anniversary of priesthood on June 18, 1974 at a Mass in St. Michael's Church, Olympia, concelebrated with Father Blaise Feeney, O.S.B., director of Religious Education, St. Michael's Parish, and Associate Pastors Father Thomas Hesselbrock, Jean Chapman and Jack Walmesley.

Interior of the new Temple De Hirsch Sinai, Seattle. In the center is the Holy Ark in the form of the Ten Commandments symbolizing the discipline of Torah. The wall is of 25 colored prismatic panels. These symbolize the Holy Days and festivals.

Rabbi Levine presides as a Bar Mitzvah boy, Harvey Poll, reads from the Torah Scroll in the old Temple De Hirsch as his father, Harold Poll, looks on. Harvey is now president-elect of Temple De Hirsch Sinai and the attorney for Camp Brotherhood.

The Torah Scroll, open at the Ten Commandments, Exodus 20. The Scroll contains the first five books of the Jewish Bible written by hand on parchment.

Left: Rabbi Levine with daughter Lori in England. Right: The Goldsteins with whom Rabbi Levine lived in London during the blitz. His family had returned to America for safety just before World War II broke out. Rabbi lived with the Goldsteins for two years until returning to America in 1941.

The Levine family goes to college. In 1946 Lori Jean was an undergraduate at the University of Washington and Rabbi and Madeline were taking graduate courses in education.

Rabbi's daughter, Lori Jean, and family: Debbie Sue, Stephan, husband Louis Sternberg, and Lynn standing in back row beside her mother.

The new Temple De Hirsch built in 1960 with the chapel (left) built in 1974. In front is the Menorah, the seven-branch candelabrum described in the Bible as the lighting fixture of the Tabernacle.

Louis Levine, now 92, Mrs. Ida Levine Goldfine and Raphael Levine in Minneapolis August 1974 to celebrate Ida's 80th birthday.

The Jewish National Fund honored Rabbi Levine in 1966 by naming a grove of trees in Israel after him. He preferred to call this the Seattle Brotherhood Wood and for many years he and Father Treacy, who have worked so long together for brotherhood, long dreamed of going to Israel together to plant the first trees. Here Israel Consul General Sagee presents the citation as Dr. Corson and Father Treacy look on.

Left: Father Treacy with Father Dennis Wood the evening of his installation as pastor of St. Michael's Church, Olympia, September 29, 1971. Right: Father Treacy with his aunt and godmother, Mrs. Patrick Phelan, taken in Ireland in 1971.

On Father Treacy's 25th jubilee as a priest, Mrs. Reeva Levine presented a portrait she had painted of him. Here she shows the portrait to Miss Evelyn Hall and Mrs. Agnes Douglass, Father Treacy's cousin, who had come from her home in New York City for the jubilee celebrations.

They played a most significant part in a better understanding of my own role as a rabbi and aided me immeasurably in my spiritual odyssey up to now. I say "up to now" because it is yet unfinished and I know will never be finished as long as I live on earth. Through knowing Father Treacy, the dedicated and totally committed priest of his Church as I know him to be, I gained a deeper insight into the Church which helped to make him what he is. The beauty of our relationship is that it has not been one-sided as readers might be led to believe from Father Treacy's version, with me as the giver and Father Treacy as the recipient. It was a relationship in which he contributed to my spiritual growth as much as I to his. It was a relationship in which the beneficial enrichment was mutual and reciprocal, the kind of relationship that transcends all man-made patterns of sectarian differences and touches the core depth of religious communication on a level of love between human beings which God intended all of us ultimately to achieve.

This does not mean that sectarian religion is not important. It is not only important but in my opinion, inevitable. I do not believe that in any foreseeable future, all the different religions of the world will be merged into one world religion, with the same theology and forms of worship and practice. Until the races of the world, languages, cultures, habits of thought and life-styles are merged and all differences in personal growth and maturation are eradicated, I do not see the possibility of one world religion which all humanity will accept and live by. Nor do I think it would be desirable even if it were possible. The very diversity of our human family contributes to the enrichment of human life. It would contribute even more to human fulfillment and happiness if we realized our oneness as a human family bound together into an ever closer relationship on the earth by political, economic and ecological facts of survival on this planet.

So I believe that what Father Treacy and I have discovered in and through each other is a deeper appreciation of the role which sectarian religion can fulfill and become the blessing it has never fully achieved.

This was beautifully expressed by Father Treacy's speaking from the pulpit of our Temple on a Friday evening in February 1966. It was our regular Sabbath service which was not altered one iota from our normal Sabbath worship except that Father Treacy's sermon came at the end instead of in the middle of the service as was my normal practice. The large sanctuary was almost full with nearly 900 worshipers of all faiths. Father spoke about some of the far-reaching implications for ecumenism of Vatican Council II and that as a Christian he believed in the incarnation of God in Jesus who in a personal way manifested God's love and concern for human beings. For this reason, he said, he believed that it was in the person-to-person contact that we must come to know each other and love each other.

After the service many worshipers, both Christians and Jews, told me they never had felt the presence of God so overwhelmingly as in the spirit of true brotherhood which radiated throughout the service that night. Mrs. Isaac Brown, who was 92 and has since passed away, a founding member of our congregation, told Father Treacy with tears of joy that she thanked God she was privileged to live to see this day.

Pope John, of blessed memory, opened windows upon the world to the Catholic Church that had been closed for centuries. In his conception of the Church's new mission he also inspired non-Catholics of all faiths to re-examine their own sectarianism and to realize that by becoming aware that other faiths also had a portion of God's love and truth that they were not being disloyal to their own, only being enriched in their understanding of the deepest insights of their own faith. It is in that spirit that Father Treacy is an authentic disciple of Pope John, even as I believe I am true to the teachings of Judaism at its best. When I say, as I have so often said publicly in lectures and on CHALLENGE, that Judaism is the best religion in the world for me but not necessarily for a Christian, or a Hindu, or a Buddhist, I believe I speak with the authentic voice of Judaism, for I know that 2000 years ago it was said in Judaism, "The righteous among all people shall have a share in the world to come", the rabbinic way of saying all men are accepted and loved by God.

That is why we have written this book together, to show that people as different as an Irish Catholic boy born near a village in central Ireland and a Jewish boy born in a Russian ghetto, so different in ethnic origins and cultural backgrounds, so far apart in our religious faiths, so diverse in our education and experience, and so different in temperament as Father Treacy and I should have met in Seattle and have been able to overcome all our early conditioning to achieve the kind of relationship we have so inadequately tried to describe in this book. This to me is the most convincing evidence that there is a divine Providence that shapes our ends, rough hew them though we may.

Epilogue

FATHER TREACY

22

From The Daily Olympian—November 7, 1971

"I am Rabbi Levine of Seattle. Can you help get me out? I'm locked in St. Michael's Catholic rectory here in Olympia."

That's the message to the telephone company of early and nippy last Friday morning. He got help.

To explain: Rabbi Raphael Levine, retired, and for many years a panelist on the television show, CHALLENGE, last Thursday visited his panelist colleague, the Rev. William Treacy, currently pastor of St. Michael's Church here. It was the Rabbi's first visit to Father Treacy since the latter became pastor a few weeks ago—and his first overnight stay in a Catholic rectory!

The two planned a Friday morning walk, to start at 7 a.m. About 5:30 a.m. Rabbi Levine woke up and decided to make some coffee for himself against the early and brisk walking time.

Lo and behold, clad in pajamas, he found himself not in the rectory kitchen but the rectory basement or hall—and, as he entered, the door closed and locked behind him.

How to get to Father Treacy? His pajamas made the trip outside and around the rectory door formidable. He looked around and found a plug-in telephone. Hence the message to the operator.

Yes, the two long-time CHALLENGE panelists took their morning walk, after coffee!"

23 Brothers In Hope

"Brothers in Hope" aptly describes the relationship between Rabbi Levine and me. It is also the title of the 1971 yearbook on Jewish-Christian relations edited by Monsignor John M. Oesterreicher of the Institute of Judaeo-Christian Studies, Seton Hall University.

In this book Jewish scholars ask the question, "Is dialogue a necessity for Jews?" Some have maintained that Judaism is autonomous, that it does not depend in any way on the religions that grew out of it, whereas the very roots of Christianity are those of Judaism. Dr. Jacob B. Agus, Rabbi of Beth-El Congregation in Baltimore, asks: "Can we Jews achieve self-understanding without taking account of the deep imprint on Western culture of the daughter faith of Judaism? . . . And if our self-understanding must include the role of Christianity, not only in its early career within the Jewish and Greco-Roman worlds, but also its subsequent struggle for dominance within the human family as a whole, can we be content to study this phenomenon through books? Rather is it not essential for us to recognize that a living faith must be encountered as it is incarnated in its representatives?"

This distinguished Rabbi was saying in 1971 what Rabbi Levine has been saying to me since I first met him in 1960, that we must come to know people as people and not just read about them and their beliefs.

The dialogue between Jews and Christians had as its starting point the rooting out of anti-Semitism from Christianity. But we need one another. Over and over again, Rabbi Levine has preached against a paradox of organized religion, that in teaching how to attain righteousness with God we must not become

127

self-righteous. Rabbi Seymour Siegal of New York City points out the important stake Jews have in the future of Christianity. "Christianity is our ally in the bringing of morality and humanism into the affairs of men," he writes. Whenever Christianity disappears it gives way to forces that are inimical to the cause of man—which is of course the cause of Judaism."

In my years of dialogue with Rabbi Levine I have come to understand something of the road ahead and find others saying what he has repeated to me "in season and out of season". He has studied the New Testament carefully and is not afraid to quote Jesus on a television program. As a Jew he finds he is challenged by the presence of the Church to search for the core meaning of Judaism. As a Christian drawn closer to Judaism because of my friendship with the Rabbi, I feel this same challenge in probing Christianity. The new theological studies that see the Church as the "new people of God" integrally bound up with Judaism I find exciting and a cause for joy. In the past, Christian teachers too often held that the Church of the Gentiles had replaced the Jews as God's people. The tearing of the Temple veil recorded in Matthew's Gospel was regarded as the end of God's covenant with the Jews. Now as we talk about commitment and fidelity we are beginning to realize, as Paul pointed out in his letter to the Romans (c. 11), that God is faithful to His agreements and the Jewish people are still very much the object of His love.

Because some Jews like Rabbi Levine are pioneering in the study of Christianity it does not mean we are to expect a mass conversion of Jews to Christianity. This is not the goal or purpose of dialogue, nor was it the purpose of CHALLENGE. On the other hand, a fresh and new respect for Jewish theology does not mean a watering down of faith in Jesus. I believe with

Father John Pawlikowski, professor at Catholic Theological Union in Chicago, that this new understanding "must lead both Jews and Christians to admit that their faiths are limited expressions of the total religious understanding of man. Hence, in a spirit of humility and conscious of their uniqueness, they must stand ready to learn from each other as well as together from other religions. Where this learning process might someday lead, no one can predict. For the foreseeable future both Judaism and Christianity will retain their integrity as distinct religious entities." ("The Ecumenist", September-October 1971)

I have shared with Rabbi Levine books and articles by Father Edward H. Flannery, Executive Secretary of the American Bishops' Secretariat for Catholic-Jewish Relations and author of *The Anguish of the Jews*. He reviews Jules Isaac's book *Jesus and Israel* in the 1972 winter issue of "Ecumenical Studies". Jules Isaac lost his wife and family in the Holocaust and in his book traces the development of anti-Semitism to misinterpretations of the Gospel. Father Flannery concludes his review:

. . . It is not for the Christian in dialogue, I understand, to tell Jews what they can or should learn from Christianity. Rather it is for Jews to do when and as they see fit. It is a little early to take a reciprocalist view of the dialogue and ask Jews, who have so suffered from Christian hands and who are yet uncertain as to the depth of our resolve to begin anew, to undertake a eulogy of Christianity and see it somehow as an exemplar for Jews. The day will doubtless come when the years of bitterness will be acknowledged by Christians and in consequence forgotten by Jews, when Jew and Christian will approach each other in reciprocal exchange of insight and edification.

Rabbi Levine returned the review by Father Flannery with this notation beside the above paragraph: "We have been walking in this direction since 1960."

Questions raised in dialogue between Christians and Jews take us into deep theological waters, waters not too well charted or marked. As we sail into these new areas, I find myself reflecting on words spoken by Jesus to another rabbi who came to him at night because of the hostility already centered on Jesus. Jesus reminded this leading Jew, Nicodemus, "the wind blows where it pleases; you hear its sound, but you cannot tell where it comes from or where it is going. This is how it is with all who are born of the Spirit." (John 3:8)

We must be willing to be guided by the Spirit of God. I believe the Spirit enriched and enriches my life and priesthood in relation to God and man through my friendship with Rabbi Levine. And I have dared to share these reflections with you to encourage further dialogue between Jews and Christians, to invite others to follow us on this new road of genuine appreciation of one another's convictions and of mutual sharing of our spiritual gifts as men of faith who all are sons of Abraham and believe with Paul that "love is the fulfilling of the Law". (Romans 13:10)

24
Epilogue and Prologue

During our years together on television, Rabbi Levine frequently quoted a favorite Chinese proverb: "A picture is worth a thousand words"—to which he made two amendments: "an example is worth a thousand pictures and an experience is worth a thousand examples". Jerusalem is truly a holy city for both of us, and Israel, land of the Prophets and land where Jesus manifested Himself, is our common homeland; we long dreamed of a pilgrimage there together.

In 1966 the Jewish National Fund honored Rabbi Levine by naming a wood in Israel after him. Through the centuries invaders came and ravaged the land, destroying every tree and making way for serious erosion of the soil. The planting of trees and widespread experimentation with varieties of trees from all over the world is an international effort to repair the ravages of war and neglect over 2000 years. Rabbi Levine asked that the area planted in his honor not be called by his name but instead the Seattle Brotherhood Wood.

The possibility of the two of us planting trees together in Israel inspired us to make every effort to travel there together and through the planting of trees to express our appreciation and love for the land that gave food to the Prophets and people of Israel, that provided Jesus with nourishment and now was providing food and shelter to the Jews of the dispersion returning to their homeland.

From 1966 on we talked from time to time about such an ecumenical experience in the Holy Land. The management of KOMO-TV agreed to send a television crew with us making it possible to share the experience with the people of the Pacific Northwest through CHALLENGE. Dr. Fine and Rabbi Levine

131

explained the project on television and radio and recruited approximately 12 Protestants, 12 Jews and 12 Catholics from the Northwest to accompany us. On February 21, 1972 we set out together for Israel.

When Rabbi and I visited Jerusalem on the People-to-People tour in 1963, it was not possible for him to enter the section under Arab control, which included the Temple area. Now for the first time in his life he got a close look at that part of Jerusalem so dear to his people for 3000 years. And the view looked good as he stood beside his friends, the Protestant minister and the Catholic priest.

On the morning of February 23 we assembled at the Kennedy Memorial Forest for the dedication of the Seattle Brotherhood Wood that had brought us to Israel. The John F. Kennedy Memorial presides from a high mountaintop over the tree planting in an area just southwest of Jerusalem. From many miles around, the huge memorial, designed like a tree cut off in midgrowth, can be seen and the mountaintop itself with the pattern of the road winding up to the memorial appears an enormous cross-section of a tree trunk. The wind was bitter that day at the memorial but less cold on a lower mountain where Rabbi, Dr. Fine and I planted trees and the Seattle Brotherhood Wood was begun and dedicated with this prayer:

And these saplings
Which we plant before Thee this day
In the Seattle Brotherhood Wood,
Make deep their roots and wide their crown,
That they may blossom forth in peace
Amongst all the trees in Israel,
For good and for beauty.

In Israel the Christians among us came to a new and better understanding of what Israel is for Jews. To both those who believe in God and those who do not, it is home, a refuge from the barbarism inflicted on Jews through their history, a place to live in dignity and freedom. To the believer it is also the sign of God's love and care. It struck me that the faith of the modern Jewish parent has much in common with the faith of Abraham who was willing to sacrifice his only son, Isaac, because implicit in the return to Israel is the possibility that their sons will be sacrificed on the battlefield.

We Christians shared the enthusiasm and pride of our Jewish friends as we visited the tomb of Theodore Hertzl, father of the modern state of Israel, the Knesset, the magnificent Hebrew University, Haddassah Hospital for which many of them had raised money, City Hall where officials explained the problems and aspirations for all in their city, Jew and non-Jew.

We went together to Yad Vashem, the memorial to six million Jews killed in the gas chambers. The Nazis kept record of the names of all the victims and the Israeli government is now collecting data about each one so that more than just the names of these martyred members of the human family may be transmitted to future members. Seeing at Yad Vashem such evidence of the deed done to his Jewish brother, the Christian man is confronted with his part in the crucifixion of Christ. Pictures of the trains arriving with their frightened, packed human cargoes were too much for the Rabbi. We had to leave the building for fresh air.

I walked in silence with him on the grounds toward the high pylon built like a chimney and there recalled the words of the teenage Anne Frank written in hiding shortly before she was sent to the gas chamber: "I still believe that man is good at heart and that things will one day be all right".

Another part of my dream to visit Israel with the Rabbi was to walk side-by-side with him and Dr. Fine along the Via Dolorosa. We did in the regular Friday afternoon commemoration of Jesus' carrying the cross from the place of condemnation near the Temple area to Calvary. Later I asked the Rabbi what his thoughts were as he walked the Via Dolorosa with Dr. Fine and me. He said, "I was thinking first of the experience of a rabbi, a priest and a Protestant minister walking arm-in-arm on those steps hallowed by Christian tradition and to the Jews the source and symbol of so much tragedy and suffering in their lives across the last 1900 years. As I was thinking of this man Jesus walking up these steps to his death at the hands of Roman executioners, I thought also of how every prophet—both among the ancient Hebrews and among all peoples even to our own day—was misunderstood and rejected by the people of his day. Throughout history this has always been so with far-visioned trailblazers in the spiritual life of mankind who have been done to death by those who could not understand the insights which made these martyrs for God the kind of men and women they were."

We visited Jericho on the way from Jerusalem to the Dead Sea and Masada, pausing along the way as I read outside an old inn the beautiful story Jesus told about the traveler going down from Jerusalem to Jericho. The traveler, beaten and left by the roadside, was befriended and cared for not by his coreligionists but by strangers. We visited the site of ancient Jericho and as we looked down through layer after layer of history, Rabbi read the story of the Israelites crossing the Jordan to the Promised Land after their deliverance from Egypt and 40 years of wandering in the desert of Sinai. Here we stood another people—people of the 20th Century weary of wandering in disunity—looking toward the Promised Land of true brotherhood.

At Masada our Jewish friends identified with the determination of Jews against Roman armies in 69 A.D. Everywhere we saw signs of new life in a largely barren land—a kibbutz on the shore of the Dead Sea experimenting with hydroponic farming and extracting from waters that can kill only what will give life; irrigation projects that made the desert bloom; lush orchards in Northern Galilee; high-rise housing everywhere under construction in Tel Aviv. An overnight stay in Kibbutz Hagoshrim near the point where Israel, Lebanon and Syria meet gave us an experience worth a thousand examples. We talked to these Jews of Turkish descent and understood the impetus behind all the other signs of progress we had seen that week.

One clear sunny afternoon we gathered on the Mount of the Beatitudes overlooking the Sea of Galilee and Rabbi, Dr. Fine and I each read a chapter from the Sermon on the Mount. I don't think I shall ever be able to recall the Mount, the Sea of Galilee or the Sermon on the Mount without hearing Rabbi's preface to these readings: "Remember we are about to hear a Jew speaking to Jews. We cannot fully understand the Sermon on the Mount unless we are aware that the Jewish Jesus was speaking to Jews formed by the synagogue and Temple". As we listened to him enlarge on the Beatitudes and draw parallels from chapter 19 of the Book of Leviticus, we saw in greater depth what Jesus was saying to all men then and now about their great worth and sublime possibilities as co-creators with God of their own lives and of the world.

The last evening we were in Jerusalem the entire Challenge group gathered at Ecce Homo convent built over what was once a corner of the Temple area. We descended two flights of stairs to a paved area where archaeologists have discovered evidences of the Lithostrotos, the place where Pilate stood when he condemned Jesus to death by crucifixion, symbolically washing his hands to relieve himself of guilt and to show that the responsibility for the death belonged to another.

The night before He died Jesus celebrated the Passover meal with His Apostles. We Catholics believe that He instituted the priesthood and the Mass when He commissioned the Apostles to recall that last Passover meal through the use of bread and wine and that He becomes present to us in these symbols of nourishment. Preparing to offer the Mass this evening at the simple altar set on ancient cobblestones, I saw again the priest as I had seen him at the altar when I was a boy in Killasmeestia surrounded by neighbors whose faces reflected.their faith. Never did I dream then that I would be offering Mass on this spot in the company of a rabbi, a Protestant minister, Jews who had lost members of their families in the Holocaust, Protestants and Catholics who remembered the days of the Ku Klux Klan and intense religious bigotry.

Dr. Fine read the scripture lesson for the day and at the conclusion of the Mass, Rabbi Levine commented on the Gospel read from Matthew about the choice Pilate gave to the Jews between a scourged Jesus and Barabbas. He said in part: "To understand what happened we must try to understand that Barabbas to many in that crowd was no mere criminal being given a pardon by Pilate at the Passover season, but a political prisoner, a guerilla fighter, a member of the Zealots which was a militant political party dedicated to freeing Judea from Roman occupation of their country. To the crowd assembled there he was a hero, whereas to most of them, Jesus was just another itinerant preacher. How could they have known that he would someday be worshiped as the son of God?"

Earlier in the day I had been walking with the Rabbi near the Church of the Holy Sepulchre. He turned to me and said, "Father, I want to buy you a special souvenir of our visit to

Jerusalem." I thanked him but said it was not necessary. We walked a few blocks in silence and then stopped in front of a small carpenter shop where the Moslem proprietor was at work. On entering I saw a beautiful long-stemmed cup made of olive wood and showed it to the Rabbi. He said, "I once made an altar for you. Can you use this at Mass?" He purchased it and I used it for the first time at the Mass I offered that evening at the Lithostrotos.

Just before the Communion of the Mass I paused to give a greeting of peace to the congregation. The first person I turned to was Rabbi Levine and I shall never forget the joy on his face at that moment. It spoke volumes about what people can be to one another and how in walking the pilgrim way together, assisted by our differences, we can come to fuller union with God. I greeted Dr. Fine and saw tears on the faces of many as the congregation embraced us and one another.

I saw a baptism of love—a washing away of some of the terrible sins of anti-Semitism and religious bigotry through the centuries and a pledge of a new and better life when members of the human family can stand together in love with arms outstretched to embrace one another and bridge the gaps between them.